AN ALBUM OF
MAYA ARCHITECTURE

Tatiana Proskouriakoff

DOVER PUBLICATIONS, INC.
Mineola, New York

Bibliographical Note

This Dover edition, first published in 2002, is an unabridged republication of the work first published by the Carnegie Institution of Washington, Washington, D.C., in 1946.

Library of Congress Cataloging-in-Publication Data

Proskouriakoff, Tatiana, 1909–
    An album of Maya architecture / Tatiana Proskouriakoff.
       p. cm.
    Originally published: Washington, D.C. : Carnegie Institution of Washington, 1946.
    ISBN 0-486-42484-7 (pbk.)
    1. Maya architecture. 2. Mayas—Antiquities. 3. Mexico—Antiquities. 4. Central America—Antiquities. I. Title.

F1435.3.A6 P7 2002
720'.89'97415—dc21

2002031301

Manufactured in the United States of America
Dover Publications, Inc., 31 East 2nd Street, Mineola, N.Y. 11501

ACKNOWLEDGMENT

IN 1938, Dr. Linton Satterthwaite Jr., of the University Museum at Philadelphia, suggested to me that I make a perspective drawing of the acropolis at Piedras Negras. He put at my disposal all the unpublished data which the expeditions of the museum had obtained during their excavations at the site, and gave me his personal help and advice in its preparation. The project of making a series of such drawings representing various sites in the Maya area was first conceived by Dr. Sylvanus G. Morley, of the Carnegie Institution of Washington, who personally undertook to obtain financial assistance for my trip to Copan in 1939, and to Chichen Itza and the cities of the Puuc in 1940. I am deeply grateful to the anonymous contributors, who as the Friends of Copan and the Friends of Chichen Itza, responded so generously and made it possible for me to make studies at first hand of the buildings at these two sites. Without their help the project might never have been undertaken. To Dr. Morley, however, I am indebted not only for its initiation and for his successful efforts in my behalf, but also for the constant encouragement, constructive criticism, and invaluable suggestions he has offered so freely in every phase of its progress, giving generously of his time and attention to the planning of the drawings and the reading of the introduction and the original draft of the text. With equal gratitude I recall the unstinted help I have received from Dr. J. Alden Mason, curator of the American Section of the University Museum of the University of Pennsylvania, and from Dr. Linton Satterthwaite Jr., who was in charge of its expeditions to Piedras Negras from 1933 to 1940. Much unpublished material incorporated in the Piedras Negras drawings has been made available to me through the courtesy of the museum, which has also offered me the use of a drafting room and other facilities for its utilization. For Dr. Satterthwaite's concrete help in the interpretation of the data and for his advice and encouragement I can never adequately express my thanks.

Among my colleagues of the Carnegie Institution of Washington, I have also met throughout with the sort of cooperation that brings to any project the benefits of a wider scope of experience than rests in an individual author. Briefly I want to mention their specific contributions, but not before expressing my particular appreciation of the unfailing interest of Dr. A. V. Kidder, under whose supervision the book took shape and from whose suggestions, in fact, it largely derives its present form. To Mr. Gustav Strömsvik I am indebted for much information from his deep fund of knowledge about the ruined structures of Copan, and for numerous courtesies which facilitated my trip to the site and helped to make my visit there pleasant and worth while. Mr. Karl Ruppert made available to me the results of his work at Xpuhil and on the Mercado at Chichen Itza, which were unpublished when the drawings were made. Dr. H. E. D. Pollock has helped me by criticisms and suggestions dealing with the restoration of buildings in the Puuc area, and by providing me with most of the data on which they are based. To Mr. A. Ledyard Smith I owe the publication of the series of drawings depicting Structure A-V at Uaxactun, which originally were designed for his report. Mr. Edwin M. Shook's excellent plans of this structure are the basis of the restorations, and I am also indebted to Mr. Shook for the difficult trip he made in 1941 to Tikal to obtain measurements and notes which have made possible a restoration of Temple II.

Dr. Kenneth J. Conant, of the Department of Architecture in the Graduate School of Design, Harvard University, and Mr. Henry R. Shepley have both contributed many helpful suggestions, and I am grateful to Mrs. W. H. Harrison not only for her careful reading of the text but also for her ready and sympathetic attention to problems outside the scope of her official duties as editor of the Division of Historical Research.

Many friends here and in Middle America, by their kindness and courtesy, have helped to make my task lighter and more pleasant. I want to thank them all for their interest, which has been a constant incentive, and which is inextricably fused with my own efforts in the making of every page of this book.

CONTENTS

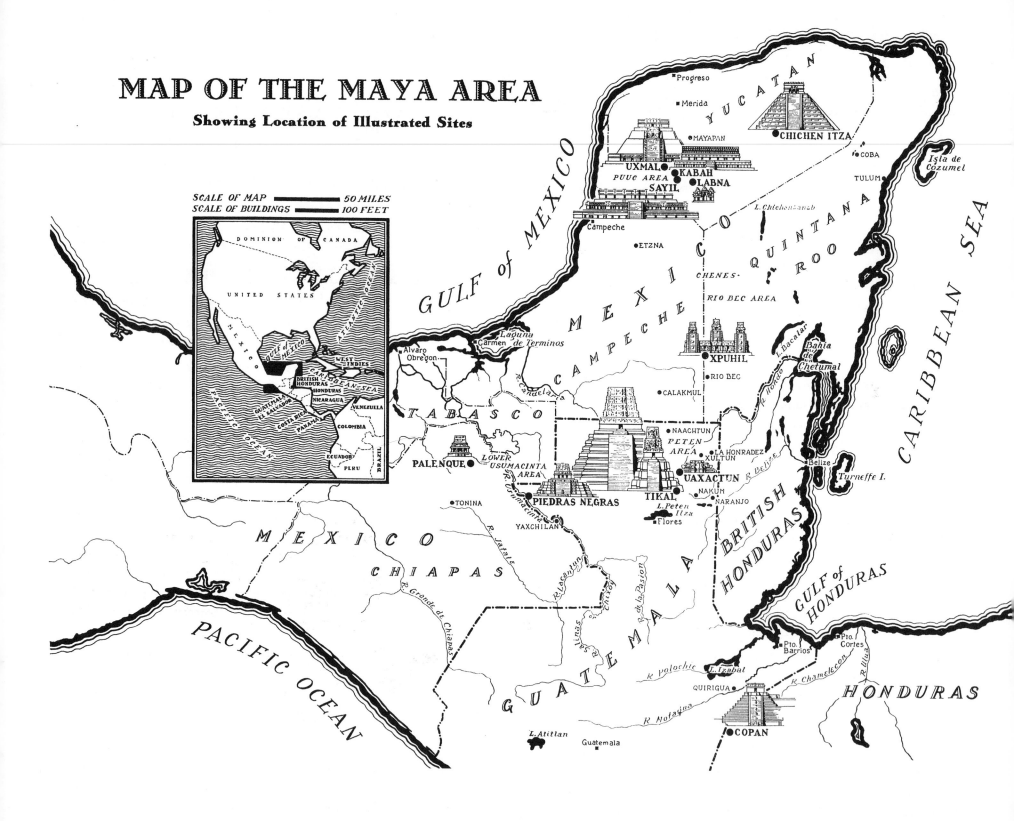

MAP OF THE MAYA AREA
Showing Location of Illustrated Sites

SCALE OF MAP — 50 MILES
SCALE OF BUILDINGS — 100 FEET

DOMINION OF CANADA

UNITED STATES

ATLANTIC OCEAN

MEXICO

GULF of MEXICO

WEST INDIES

PACIFIC OCEAN

BRITISH HONDURAS
HONDURAS
NICARAGUA
GUATEMALA
EL SALVADOR
COSTA RICA
PANAMA

CARIBBEAN SEA

VENEZUELA

COLOMBIA

ECUADOR

PERU

BRAZIL

GULF of MEXICO

Progreso
Merida
YUCATAN
MAYAPAN
CHICHEN ITZA
COBA
Isla de Cozumel
TULUM
UXMAL
PUUC AREA
KABAH
SAYIL
LABNA
Campeche
ETZNA
L. Chichenkanab
QUINTANA ROO
CHENES-
RIO BEC AREA
MEXICO
CAMPECHE
XPUHIL
RIO BEC
L. Bacalar
Bahia de Chetumal
R. Hondo

Laguna Carmen de Terminos
Alvaro Obregon
R. Candelaria
TABASCO
CALAKMUL
NAACHTUN
PETEN AREA
LA HONRADEZ
XULTUN
UAXACTUN
R. Belize
Belize
Turneffe I.

CARIBBEAN SEA

PALENQUE
LOWER USUMACINTA AREA
R. Usumacinta
TIKAL
L. Peten Itza
NAKUM
NARANJO
Flores
BRITISH HONDURAS

TONINA
PIEDRAS NEGRAS
R. Lacantun
YAXCHILAN
MEXICO
CHIAPAS
R. Grande de Chiapas
R. Jatate
R. Salinas
R. Chixoy
R. de la Pasion
GUATEMALA
GULF of HONDURAS
Pto. Barrios
Pto. Cortes

PACIFIC OCEAN

L. Atitlan
Guatemala
R. Motagua
QUIRIGUA
L. Izabal
R. Polochic
R. Chameleon
R. Ulua
COPAN
HONDURAS

INTRODUCTION

EARLY in the sixteenth century, when Spanish conquerors were exploring the mainland of the New World, Tenochtitlan, the largest Aztec city of the valley of Mexico, was the dominant center of civilization in Middle America. The fame of its tall temples, its active military organization, and particularly its wealth of silver and gold created a sensation among ambitious adventurers, and many Spanish chronicles of the period contain vivid descriptions of its splendor. In contrast, the peninsula of Yucatan, occupied by less aggressive peoples speaking the Maya language, was distant hinterland to the wealthier Mexican cities. Only the more astute and curious of the European newcomers noted the many disused buildings and abandoned cities in this area, and perceived that the land had once enjoyed a level of civilization that certainly rivaled, if it did not surpass, that of the Mexicans. Friar Diego de Landa, who has left an excellent account of the life and customs of the Maya Indians of his day, expresses sincere admiration of these monuments of a forgotten era: "If the number, grandeur and beauty of its buildings were to count toward the attainment of renown and reputation in the same way as gold, silver and riches have done for other parts of the Indies, Yucatan would have become as famous as Peru and New Spain have become, so many, in so many places, and so well built of stone are they, it is a marvel; the buildings themselves, and their number are the most outstanding thing that has been discovered in the Indies."

Landa attempted to learn the history of the ancient cities by questioning the Indians, but the accounts he gathered were sketchy and confused. There were still at that time many native hieroglyphic manuscripts in Yucatan, and perhaps they contained more authentic historical data; but the knowledge of hieroglyphic writing among the Indians was restricted to the nobility and the priesthood and very little of it was imparted to the Spaniards. Moreover, Bishop Landa himself mistrusted the source of these writings and took great care that no one should ever again consult them. "We found a great number of books in these letters," he relates, "and since they contained nothing but superstitions and falsehoods of the devil we burned them all, which they took most griev-

ously, and which gave them great pain." In the light of the slightly more tolerant tenor of our era, it seems a pity that so much of Maya lore, history, and science literally went up in smoke at this auto-da-fé.

From the only three codices that survived and turned up years later in European libraries, we can now see that not all Maya writing was falsehood and superstition. Much of it was accurate astronomical computation that dealt with the length of the solar year and the lunations, the occurrence of eclipses, and the periods of revolution of the planets. Unfortunately, the structure of the hieroglyphic characters is still not clearly understood and passages of straight text cannot be deciphered, but both the codices and the inscriptions on stone contain numerical data which are beginning to reveal that the ancient Maya savants were uncommonly skillful and ambitious astronomers. They had an elaborate calendrical system, so devised that they could reckon to the day periods of time comprising many thousands of years, and so unequivocally recorded that it remains only to discover a single point of contact between their calendar and ours in order to translate all Maya dates into Gregorian equivalents. Several correlations have been proposed, differing from each other by periods of about 260 years or its multiples, but authorities still disagree on their relative merits. Gregorian dates which occur in this book have been calculated by the correlation currently in favor with most students, that based on the original work of J. T. Goodman, which was later amended by J. Martinez-Hernandez and further modified by J. Eric S. Thompson.

According to this system, the earliest undisputed date in Maya history, if we except those dates which were clearly in the past when inscribed and were probably legendary, is 8.14.3.1.12, or September 18, A.D. 320. It is carved on a small plaque or pendant of jade known as the Leyden Plate. On its reverse side is a human figure elaborately dressed in ceremonial attire. The style of the design is undoubtedly early, but neither archaic nor crude, and we can scarcely ascribe it to the formative phases of Middle American civilization when distinctively Maya traits were being crystallized from the amorphous content of ruder cultures. Of these early phases we know regrettably little as yet. One fact only seems clear: that the Maya had been occupying for many centuries the regions where their civilization later flourished, and that although individual traits may have been introduced from time to time from other areas, the integration of their distinctive culture was continuous and took place in situ, without major disturbances or shifts of population. At the time of the Leyden Plate inscription, its chief characteristics were already clearly defined. It was no longer a primitive or barbaric culture. Its artistic tradition was fixed and mature, and expressed itself in the depiction of an impressive ritual that was to permeate Maya activities for many centuries to come.

Beginning about A.D. 328, the practice of erecting large stone monuments, inscribed with hieroglyphic texts containing usually one or more calendrical notations, characterizes the period known as the Old Empire. Many of these ancient monuments or stelae are now broken and eroded. For centuries they have been lying neglected among the ruins, where the torrential rains and the avid roots of the dense vegetation are destroying their delicate carving and obscuring the intricate detail of their design. Some, however, almost miraculously have escaped the ravages of nature and have preserved their carving virtually intact. Almost invariably they depict the same traditional motif—a lordly figure of some priest or chieftain wearing elaborate insignia of office, an intricate costume of finely embroidered material, ornaments of shell or jade, and a lofty headdress of flowing plumes. Details are reproduced in stone with meticulous care, and the naturalism and beauty of some of these sculptures compare favorably with the finest examples of sculpture in classical antiquity.

Since the earliest stelae are found in northeastern Guatemala, it has been generally assumed that the stela cult developed in this region and gradually spread to other areas. Recently this conclusion has been challenged by the discovery in southern Veracruz of monuments which may date from very early times. It is not clear, however, whether the unusual character of their dates indicates an early type of notation, or whether it implies an altogether different method of counting time. Maya archaeologists are finding themselves in that discomfiting but stimulating phase in the progress of their studies when a number of such new discoveries, coming into conflict with formerly accepted theories, have still to be appraised and assimilated. The latest researches have tended to show that civilization as evidenced by large constructions was, even in pre-Old Empire times, far more widespread than previously supposed, and that the southern Maya cities enjoyed a freer contact with other areas at this time than in subsequent periods. The great pyramids of the Sun and the Moon at Teotihuacan in the valley of Mexico were probably built during the formative periods of Maya civilization—certainly not later than early Old Empire times. The contemporary ceramics of the two regions show many forms in common, indicating their close cultural contact.

In the middle period of the Old Empire, we can perceive a growing tendency of the southern Maya area to become more uniform within itself and at the same time more sharply differentiated and isolated from adjacent regions. More and more cities adopted the practice of erecting stelae, and a more complex social organization is reflected in ever more ambitious architectural projects. At this time, sites which formerly had diverse lunar calendars accepted a standard method of recording lunations, a fact which suggests that a closer political integration of the southern Maya area might have served as an impetus to the remarkable advances in the arts and sciences which followed and which culminated in the brilliant century between A.D. 700 and 800.

Although the integration of Maya culture seems to imply a concentration of political power, it is hard to say whether this should be conceived as a true empire, or whether the same results could have been accomplished by a peaceful alliance of small independent states. It is notable that there are almost no evidences of strife in this period. There are no fortified towns and very few motifs in sculpture that can be construed as even conventionalized representations of war. A small rope-bound figure of a prisoner frequently occurs on Maya stelae, but in his stripped and abject condition he seems to be rather the victim of the ceremonial practice of human sacrifice than a fit adversary for the stately and dignified central figure.

The formal tenor of all the carvings and their elaborate symbolism, which scarcely changes with the passing centuries, lead us to believe that Maya society was strongly theocratic, ruled by an exclusive and a conservative priesthood. Such an organization would account for the high degree of achievement in artistic and intellectual fields coexisting with a very primitive technology. The Maya had no metals. Their tools were made of stone, wood, bone, or shell. There were no draft animals, and the principle of the wheel, basic to the simplest engineering devices, was unknown. Maya cities had no factories, no crowded streets of commerce, no concentrated slums. Instead, there were broad open plazas, surrounded by small but ornate temples, towering on high terraced foundations, and groups of long, low narrow buildings, which in our ignorance of their various functions we class together as palaces, enclosing small rectangular courts. There were also sweat houses for the treatment of disease and for ceremonial purification, ball courts on which teams contended for athletic honors, and many other formal stone structures which made up the centers of civic life. Ordinary houses and even large residences were built, as a rule, of perishable materials and have left few traces. The small mounds that mark their remains tend to cluster around paved courts and to spread out over a large area in ever-thinning suburbs, so that it is difficult to describe the limits of a city or to estimate the number of its inhabitants. The great number of sites, however, which flourished in the prosperous eighth century, and their large constructions, imply in themselves a considerable population in many districts of the Maya area which are now almost entirely uninhabited.

What happened to all these people, why they abandoned their cities, why all their great civilization came to nothing, is a mystery that challenges our understanding of the forces that shape human societies. The facile explanation of moral degeneration followed by military defeat and ultimate conquest by more barbaric tribes is not convincing, for apparently no foreign people invaded the domain of the Maya or settled in the areas which they abandoned. It was once believed that some physical calamity drove the people in a mass migration into northern Yucatan, where they settled and continued their cultural progress. Such a theory, however, finds little corroborative evidence in archaeology. Nevertheless, though it is conceivable that the disappearance of the population may have been a gradual process, the catastrophically sudden extinction of the arts can be explained only in the terms of some widespread and unforeseen disaster that afflicted most southern Maya cities soon after A.D. 800. Before the close of the next century, apparently all the great cities of the Maya in the Peten and the southern areas were already being invaded by the forests and falling to ruin.

In Yucatan, to the north, the chronology of events is less certain, for here the custom of erecting dated monuments was not so generally practiced. At least some cities survived longer than those of the south. At one time, a wave of influence from central Mexico showed promise of inaugurating a renaissance of culture, expressed in many ambitious building projects at the site of Chichen Itza; but the new style of architecture never spread very widely. Possibly together with the artistic and religious notions of the Toltec, whose capital in Tula, Hidalgo, shows striking similarities to the Yucatan remains of this period, were introduced also the warlike traditions and barbarous practices characteristic of Mexican peoples. Conflict broke out between the cities, and for several centuries the country was devastated by a series of violent interurban wars. Mayapan, a walled city of the last turbulent period, fell to its enemies in 1441, and after its destruction, no effort was made to reoccupy the old sites or to revive the arts of masonry architecture and sculpture. At this time, when the lusty and barbarous Aztec were subjecting the valley of Mexico to the power of their glittering capital Tenochtitlan, the Maya people were divided into a number of small sporadically warring tribes, and the Spanish conquest, which in Mexico ruthlessly destroyed the promise of a virile culture, fell only as a final coup de grâce on the moribund civilization of the Maya.

In the four centuries which followed, the Maya, living under the dominance of European culture, have shared little in its advantages and have absorbed few of its essential traits. With the exception of some stubborn tribes that doggedly preserve their isolation in the trackless forest, most Maya have accepted the Catholic religion. At times their church rites appear somewhat eclectic, and local saints are likely to exhibit startling features of a pagan ancestry, but the people are unaware of the divergent sources of their beliefs, which have long since been blended in a faith, deep rooted and sincere. Other cultural gifts have been received with more conscious gratitude: notably some domestic animals, the gasoline-tin of so many uses, and the ubiquitous machete, a huge steel knife manufactured chiefly in Connecticut. Often it is the only factory-made tool and the only weapon that they possess. Though they are farmers, they use no plow but, with the aid of a pointed stick, drop grains of corn into the ground. Their thatched houses are built without nails; their few kitchen utensils are local wares of pottery and gourds; and, though in most sections of the country store-bought materials have now replaced homewoven cloth, in highland Guatemala the native textile industry still flourishes and each village is distinguished by the design of the colorful huipils worn by its women.

One can readily believe that in ancient times, families in rural districts lived very much as they do today. But in this simple life we can perceive no traces of the higher intellectual attainments of the past. All that has vanished like breath from a mirror.

It is somewhat disturbing to our complacent faith in constant progress to realize that the higher elements of a culture can be so evanescent and that they can so completely disappear, leaving intact only a bare foundation of traits essential for getting a living. Undoubtedly the weakness of Maya civilization lay in its spirituality and in the fact that its higher intellectual activities, finding no directly practical application, were bound up with the destiny of a numerically insignificant group of theocrats, artists, and scholars, whose extinction at a stroke reduced life to a very primitive level. The cities served not as foci of industry but as centers to provide the ruling caste with opportunities for theological and scientific discourse, for the elaboration of architectural and sculptural art, and for the development of gorgeous religious ritual. They were not really essential to the life of the masses, and it can well be imagined that with the still unexplained passing of the class that created them, they were rapidly abandoned.

Today, large tracts of forest are unpeopled, and a traveler in the Peten district of northern Guatemala must make his way on foot or on muleback, hacking with his machete at the fast-growing vines that constantly strive to obliterate the man-made trail. He may thus pass through the very heart of a once populous city unaware that some sharp little rise he crosses, which seems nothing more than a curious whim of nature, is in fact the ruin of some ancient edifice. It requires a conscious attention to realize the vastness of the change that has taken place, and more than a concentrated effort to visualize the scene as it might have appeared more than a thousand years ago, to see the busy, prosperous cities stripped once more of vegetation and debris and of the aura of decay and antiquity that clings so tenaciously to all ruined and abandoned buildings.

This volume of drawings presents restorations of single buildings and of parts of ancient Maya cities, and is designed especially for those who wish to get a general impression of the architecture without laboring through scientific reports or drawing too heavily upon an imagination prejudiced by greater familiarity with better-known styles. In order to create more direct visual images than most of us can construct from the reading of sections and plans, the subjects are shown in perspective plotted from the most accurate measurements available, so that the influence of the artist's personal predisposition is eliminated as far as possible. In a few instances, lines have been slightly rectified, and some freehand correction has been applied to distortions produced by wide angles of sight, but with these negligible exceptions, the views are the result of an entirely mechanical method of projection. Facing each plate is a line sketch, showing approximately the present condition of the ruin and so indicating how much reliance can be placed on its restoration. The parts of a building which still stand substantially in their original position are drawn in solid line. Broken lines show ruined or buried features which have a counterpart elsewhere on the same structure, or fallen elements whose approximate original position can be reasonably deduced from the general nature of the design. Whatever is less certain and has been restored merely by analogy with other buildings at the same site or by surmise based on habitual building practices of the Maya, is either entirely omitted from these sketches, or is indicated lightly by the outline of existing debris. At this point the observer should feel entirely free to disagree with the suggested restoration and to revise it to the satisfaction of his own judgment.

The attempt to base all restorations on sufficient and reasonably valid evidence has rigidly restricted the choice of subject and, as a result, this group of drawings makes no pretense to be a full representation of Maya architecture. Many large parts of the Maya area are still practically unexplored, and accurate data are available only from a few of the better-known sites. Moreover, it is only natural that examples of early styles are rarely found without major excavation, and even when so discovered they are usually too fragmentary to permit restoration. Consequently, the series of buildings depicted is heavily overweighted in favor of the later styles, particularly those which employed stone decoration, for only vague traces of the more commonly used stucco now remain.

That we can trace at all the development of building practices and architectural design is largely due to the fact that the Maya seldom razed to the ground a building fallen into disuse, but found it easier, it seems, to bury it completely under masonry which would serve as a foundation for new construction. Large excavations are necessary to find and unearth the earlier structures, and so far we have few examples of building sequences on which to base historical conclusions. No one, however, can fail to note that the technique of making and using plaster and mortar of burnt lime played a supremely important part in Maya architecture and influenced not only its structural forms but also the character of its design and ornament. In his report on The Temple of the Warriors at Chichen Itza, Earl Morris describes the method of burning lime which has come down from preconquest times and is common today in Yucatan. No kiln is used in the process. The limestone is burned on a huge cylindrical pile of timber, which requires a vast amount of labor to cut and considerable skill to construct in such a way that combustion of the stone and wood is complete and a minimum of impurities remains in the product. After the lime is burned, it is left exposed for a considerable length of time before it is mixed with water and temper and is ready for use. In Yucatan, sascab, a white earth formed of the harder particles of eroded limestone, is used as temper, but in regions where it is not available other earths or finely crushed limestone are substituted. In view of the primitive tools the Maya had for felling and transporting timber, the amount of mortar they were able to produce for their constructions is really amazing. No doubt the development of Maya architecture followed closely improvements in the fundamental process of lime burning. Probably at first lime was used sparingly, only as a surface finish to provide an impermeable and smooth coating for plazas, open platforms, and the masonry substructures of perishable buildings. Its use eliminated the necessity of careful cutting and laying of stone in terrace walls and provided an excellent medium for decoration, of which the Maya took full advantage to develop their superb arts of mural painting and of stucco sculpture. Even in the later carvings of stone, one can sense in the predominance of undulating lines, in the absence of sharp corners, and in the constant combination of straight line and curve, the persistent influence of a plastic medium applied to rectilinear architectural form.

Elaborate substructures for important temples, called "pyramids" because their terracing approximates a truncated pyramidal shape, already had become a fixed tradition before the building of free-standing masonry walls was attempted. Almost certainly, the construction of buildings roofed with masonry was a relatively late development, given impetus by the adaptation of lime for structural purposes. The course of this new development is so sharply in contrast with the evolution of Old World styles that we find it difficult to speak of Maya buildings in traditional architectural terms. The so-called "vault" of the Maya, for example, is neither a vault in the true sense nor a true "corbel vault" as it is often called. It is a unique form of construction, taking advantage of principles of stone arrangement, while at the same time relying heavily on the strength of mortar for its support. Many early examples, as well as some in regions where a weak mortar was used, as at Copan, may indeed be classed as true corbels; they are formed by overlapping courses of stone, each projecting farther into the room until the intervening space is narrow enough to be spanned by single slabs of stone. Even such vaults, however, tend to be built with a generous use of mortar, and the invariable habit of using cut masonry only on the surface and leaving the core a mass of rubble and mortar, produced various techniques of vault building which have no exact parallels elsewhere. The whole direction of progress veers away from the discovery of such principles as in the Old World produced the true arch, and cut stone progressively loses its structural importance as the essentially monolithic core assumes more and more the burden of the major stresses. Finally, facing stone becomes no more than a veneer of thin slabs, and its structural uselessness is sharply brought out when with time and neglect it begins to fall, leaving the inner hearting still supporting a heavy masonry vault. The type of vault stone usually associated with such construction is simply the result of leaving a tenon on the lower edge of a thin veneer stone. In some measure, this tenon tends to throw the center of gravity of the stone back into the hearting and allows it to be weighted down with rubble, but the surface it provides for the adherence of mortar is even more important. Such stones are usually tilted slightly downward, and their upper edges are sharp, providing no bearing surface for the stones immediately above, so that all their weight rests directly on rubble, and slipping is prevented only by the adhesive property of mortar.

With this and other no less original techniques, the Maya achieved considerable progress in design, succeeded in lightening the heavy masonry masses they were at first obliged to use in vaulted buildings, and increased substantially the width of rooms and openings. Nevertheless, the limitations that vault construction imposed are clearly reflected in all architectural styles, for although thatch roofs and roofs of wooden beams capped with mortar and stone were used simultaneously with the vault, the latter was preferred at most sites for important constructions.

Rooms tend to be narrow and rectangular, with few openings, and buildings generally follow a rigid pattern of design. Composition in mass is achieved by variation in the size, shape, and arrangement of substructures, elaborated by stairways occasionally so steep that even a curious tourist sometimes hesitates to climb their formidable ascent. The building proper usually stands on a smaller platform which closely follows the outline of its plan. Its walls (the lower zone) most often are plain, with simple rectangular openings, but above the "medial molding," set at about the level of the spring line of the vault, is an uninterrupted entablature (the upper zone), which often carries intricate decoration of grotesque masks, human figures, and geometric forms. A second molding (the cornice) completes the façade to the level of the cap of the roof,

which is constructed of concrete and is gently rounded or sloped to shed the heavy tropical rains or is drained by sculptured gargoyles. In some styles, decorative elements are placed on the roof to form an openwork parapet, but more often ornament is carried aloft on tall roof combs, which may be merely single walls with perforated or stucco decoration or thick masses of masonry containing tiny interior chambers.

Within this almost invariable pattern, the Maya builders managed to achieve a variety of satisfying compositions by the ingenious distribution of ornament and by the use of stairways and masses of masonry of diverse forms. Rooms were seldom directly superimposed but when raised on high solid foundations they sometimes give the effect of several stories. Striking, and yet disappointing to those who expect to find in antiquity an aspiration for the grandiose, is the small scale of the functional units of Maya structures. Doorways, for instance, seem to our unaccustomed eye disproportionately low, for they were designed for the short stature of the Maya, whose average height scarcely exceeds five feet. However, with allowances for this peculiarity of scale, the specialized functions of buildings, and the incomprehensible symbolism of ornament, it is surprising that this civilization, which apparently developed entirely independently of inspirations from the Old World, nevertheless produced artistic forms which can evoke in us an aesthetic response and which share with other more familiar styles certain qualities of design and composition which seem to have universal validity.

It is such common characteristics of otherwise widely divergent cultures, rather than their more striking contrasts, that encourage in students of history the constant effort to discover some principle of social progress and regression which would be generally applicable and which eventually might help us to understand more clearly the mounting problems confronting our own society. In our time, to all but a few determined visionaries, such an aim seems vastly remote, but it is in itself more than enough if the study of antiquities brings with it an appreciation of the accomplishments of other races and if the realization of the potentialities of obscure peoples who, like the Maya, are at present insignificant and inert, helps to keep alive the hope that under happier conditions, all nations may share equally in a common fund of culture and may equally contribute to its advance.

The quotations which have been cited in the opening paragraphs are from Diego de Landa's RELACIONES DE LAS COSAS DE YUCATAN, translated by William Gates in YUCATAN BEFORE AND AFTER THE CONQUEST BY FRIAR DIEGO DE LANDA (1937). Landa's book contains more first-hand information on the Maya Indians of conquest times than all other sources put together, and Gates's version of it captures the quaint style of the ancient chronicler and makes delightful reading. The more recent translation (1941) by Alfred M. Tozzer is provided with copious and informative annotations and is recommended for more detailed study.

The references which appear on the title pages of the plates deal specifically with the subjects portrayed, but are not intended to cover even approximately all available information. They are selected merely to direct the reader who has some doubt or question about a given structure to the source in which he is most likely to find the data he needs. By way of general reading, no one interested in Maya ruins and their exploration can afford to miss the accounts of the travels of John L. Stephens, INCIDENTS OF TRAVEL IN CENTRAL AMERICA, CHIAPAS AND YUCATAN (1841) and INCIDENTS OF TRAVEL IN YUCATAN (1843). They are illustrated with steel engravings by F. Catherwood, whose drawings are as remarkably accurate as they are attractive. ARCHAEOLOGICAL STUDIES AMONG THE ANCIENT CITIES OF MEXICO (1895-97) by W. H. Holmes is also good reading and contains panoramas of several Maya sites, giving a bird's-eye view of their general layout. George Oakley Totten's MAYA ARCHITECTURE (1926) is brief but comprehensive in its discussion and features photographs and color plates. A GLIMPSE AT GUATEMALA (1899) by A. P. and A. C. Maudslay, THE ANCIENT CITIES OF THE NEW WORLD (1887) by Claude Joseph Désiré Charnay, TRIBES AND TEMPLES (1926-27) by Frans Blom, the MEMOIRS OF THE PEABODY MUSEUM OF AMERICAN ARCHAEOLOGY AND ETHNOLOGY, and the monographs and shorter papers issued by the Carnegie Institution of Washington are but a few of the many volumes in which the reader can find both reliable data on Maya antiquities and interesting accounts of travel and exploration. The classic source of dependable measured drawings and illustrations of many Maya buildings and monuments is the BIOLOGIA CENTRALI-AMERICANA, Archaeology (1889-1902) by A. P. Maudslay, comprising one volume of text and four volumes of illustrations. The Secretario de Educacion Publica of Mexico has published comprehensive surveys of Maya sites in Mexico: ESTUDIO ARQUITECTONICO DE LAS RUINAS MAYAS (1928) by Federico E. Mariscal and ESTUDIO ARQUITECTONICO COMPARATIVO DE LOS MONUMENTOS ARQUEOLOGICOS DE MEXICO (1928) by Ignacio Marquina are so well illustrated that they are of great interest even to students who cannot read the Spanish text. All important, known sites of the Peten region of Guatemala are briefly described in THE INSCRIPTIONS OF PETEN (1937-38) by Sylvanus Griswold Morley. This work contains a vast amount of information of general interest, although its detailed analysis of the inscriptions is designed for experts. The casual reader who is interested in the Maya calendar and sciences may prefer to consult AN INTRODUCTION TO THE STUDY OF THE MAYA HIEROGLYPHS (1915) by the same author.

1

UAXACTUN, GUATEMALA

Structure E-VII sub

A COMPLETE description of this structure and its excavation may be found in UAXACTUN, GUATEMALA, GROUP E—1926-1931 (1937) by O. G. and E. B. Ricketson.

The motif below is Stela 20 of Uaxactun.

UAXACTUN
Structure E-VII sub

Uaxactun, in the heart of the Maya Old Empire, is buried in the dense, tropical forests of northeastern Peten. It is only one of many sites in this region which contains greater and more spectacular ruins, but it is of particular interest to the archaeologist because among its monuments are the earliest stelae yet discovered in the Maya area, as well as one of the latest. The Carnegie Institution began excavations at Uaxactun in 1926, and the hope that a city of such long occupation would yield examples of early architecture was amply rewarded when a trench through the badly ruined Pyramid E-VII uncovered a huge stucco face, almost perfectly preserved under later masonry. Further digging revealed that this was one of eighteen grotesque heads that decorate the stairways of the small pyramid now known as E-VII sub. Associated pottery finds indicate that this pyramid is very old—older, in fact, than the earliest stelae. It was probably intended to support a temple constructed of wood and thatch, for in the upper platform there were originally four deep post holes, which were later filled and smoothed over with plaster, as if the building had been razed, and its substructure adapted for outdoor ceremonies.

The pyramid is roughly square, with stairways on all four sides, but the upper platform has only one stairway and is higher at the rear than at the front, resembling in form the building platforms of later temples, built entirely of masonry. A striking feature of the construction is the irregularity of its shape: its grossly inaccurate angles and proportions. The facing stone is very roughly cut, laid horizontally, and covered with a thick coat of plaster. The whole looks less like a masonry structure than like a form carelessly modeled from some more plastic substance or cast in a rough mold. In spite of the crudity of workmanship, however, its well-defined design and the use of decorative elements which remain characteristic of Maya art throughout its entire history, clearly imply an established architectural tradition, and one which awaited only increased technological skill to reach full flower.

There is rude vigor in the execution of the two motifs of its ornament. One, in spite of its battered condition, can tentatively be identified as a simplified version of the serpent. The other is anthropomorphic, though to call it man or

deity is perhaps to tempt biased interpretation. It is better described noncommittally as a mask, the favorite motif of decoration in all subsequent Maya styles. The significance of masks is obscure, and in their variations they exhibit a gamut of human and animal features which is difficult to unravel. Even if in time we discover a meaning in their complicated attributes, we can never be sure that this meaning was intended by the artist. It is quite conceivable that, with constant repetition, formerly significant designs become merely abstract elements of composition, and many grotesqueries may be the result of an arbitrary mixture of traits from widely different sources. If the masks did possess a purposeful significance, we must seek even earlier examples than those of E-VII sub to discover whether this already conventional form once had a more naturalistic prototype that would permit us to give it a name.

2
TIKAL, GUATEMALA
Temple II

A PLAN and section, photographs, and a description are published in EXPLORATIONS IN THE DEPARTMENT OF PETEN, GUATEMALA (1911-1913) by Teobert Maler. The restoration is based partly on this report and partly on unpublished measurements and notes taken at the site by E. M. Shook in 1941.

The head of the Maya priest is restored from fragments of carved wooden beams found in Temple II.

TIKAL
Temple II

TIKAL is one of the largest and one of the least accessible of ancient Maya cities. Its massive temples tower above the forest that envelops and conceals countless lesser buildings, still unexplored. For many decades archaeologists have dreamed of the exciting possibilities offered by the excavation of this spectacular city, a task that would require years of effort even by a large and well-equipped expedition. The lack of a dependable source of water supply near Tikal is one of the many obstacles that have prevented intensive exploration even of the surface remains, and, although many have visited the site, few have stayed there long enough to take adequate measurements and notes of the buildings. Detailed and reliable information is scanty. This restoration of Temple II is presented with great hesitation, for it is based on insufficient and conflicting data. It is included in this series only because other examples of its type are even less well documented, and because it represents the crowning development of the temple in Old Empire times, and the composition of its mass alone may serve to illustrate the effect which the Maya builders aimed to attain. In 1941 Mr. Edwin M. Shook, of the Carnegie Institution, visited the site and obtained accurate measurements of the building itself, the platform on which it is built, and the standing portions of the roof comb. Except for the stucco decoration, which is largely destroyed, the restoration of these features is probably substantially correct. The form of the terraces of the pyramid, however, is very uncertain, as well as the exact slope of the steep stairway, which can be seen now only as a ruined mass of stone. Mr. Shook's work at Tikal was hampered by unseasonable rains, and the short period of his stay prevented his taking more than very cursory notes on the details of the substructure. These notes disagree both with the drawings presented by Maler and with the model constructed under the supervision of Dr. Herbert J. Spinden, in the Museum of Natural History in New York. In some respects, Mr. Shook's notes find confirmation in photographs, but one important feature, the existence of a low plinth or projecting molding at the bottom of each terrace wall, remains in question.

Of the five great temples at Tikal, Temple II is the smallest. The largest, Temple IV, is more than two hundred and twenty-five feet in over-all height, and is sketched on the accompanying map of the Maya area to emphasize the massive composition of Peten architecture in contrast to that of adjacent regions.

The actual room space of these temples is very small in comparison with the thickness of masonry which surrounds them, and their vaults are very high and steep. A number of lintels that spanned the doorways are still preserved. They are made of the hard, heavy wood of the sapote tree and some are beautifully decorated in the formal, ornate, but sensitively naturalistic style of the greatest period of Maya art. If we accept the chronological evidence of these lintels, which, however, may have been carved years after the erection of the buildings, we must conclude that the religious architecture of Tikal remained extremely conservative. Experiments in vault construction and variations of plan were impeded by the weight of the ponderous roof combs, and interior space was sacrificed to the effect of height and grandeur. No doubt the religious cult of the time presented to the populace an august spectacle, but reserved its secret rites and sciences for the privileged few who were instructed in its mysteries. The forbidding temples seem to express the exalted aloofness of the priesthood that ruled this great city.

3

PALENQUE, CHIAPAS

Shrine in the Temple of the Cross

SECTIONS and plans of the Temple of the Cross are published in BIOLOGIA CENTRALI-AMERICANA, Archaeology (1889-1902) by A. P. Maudslay. The combined section and perspective shown by W. H. Holmes in his ARCHAEOLOGICAL STUDIES AMONG THE ANCIENT CITIES OF MEXICO disagrees in some details with the Maudslay drawings.

The sculptured plaque is from Palace House E.

PALENQUE
Temple of the Cross

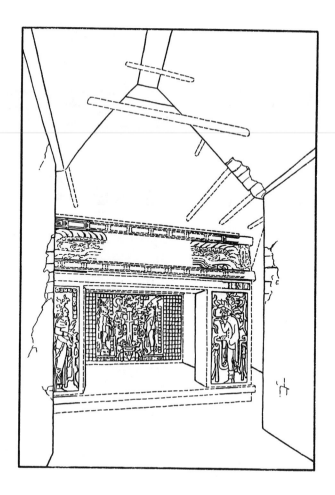

UNLIKE the ponderous temples of Tikal, those of Palenque reflect a taste which aspires to perfect proportion rather than to an overwhelming effect of sheer mass. The pyramids are not so high as to dwarf the buildings they support. Doorways are wider and more frequent, rooms are wider and vaults lower, and the roof combs, perforated to reduce their weight, are not so remotely aloft that their exquisite stucco sculpture could not conveniently be observed and enjoyed from the plaza in front of the building. The site itself, with its background of low, wooded hills seems expressly designed by nature to set off the beauty of these small temples, and a clear, swift-flowing stream that crosses the ruins is a godsend to the traveler, resigned to having his curiosity taxed by all kinds of physical discomforts. Palenque can be reached by a short ride on horseback from an air-field located at the nearby village of Palenque, but it is little visited by tourists, perhaps because it is off the regular routes of the airlines, or possibly because its main attractions are not of the sort than can be described in superlative terms.

For a number of years, the Government of Mexico has carried on excavations in the principal group at Palenque, consolidating falling masonry and reconstructing essential portions of some of the buildings to arrest their further ruin. It is hoped that this work will continue and will be extended, for Palenque is a large site, and an intensive study of its distinctive and sophisticated style cannot fail to yield rewarding results.

The Temple of the Cross is one of three which are almost identical in plan and design. It has an outer room with three wide exterior doorways which permit a view of the front chamber from below. The shrine is placed in one of the rear chambers, behind the central doorway, and is in the form of a diminutive temple. Its upper zone is ornamented with stucco, and its front wall and the rear wall of its single room were originally formed of thin slabs of stone set on edge and carved with a design of human figures and panels of hieroglyphs. These slabs have since been removed. The three which form the rear wall are now in the National Museum in Mexico City; the two on the sides of the doorway have been set into the wall of a church in Palenque village. The relief is low and delicate, emphasizing the sensitive, undulating line, which is the greatest charm of the sculptures of the great period. Distinctive of the region are the faces of the figures, with their large noses made even more prominent by sharply sloping foreheads, an effect deliberately produced by the Maya, who habitually deformed the heads of their infants by strapping them between two boards, a practice which, to judge by their cultural accomplishments, did not impair their mentality, however it may have affected their tempers. Virile youth and doddering age are clearly represented on the two front panels of the shrine. In an art which is strictly formal and depends largely on symbolism to convey its meaning, the expressiveness of these two figures is unusual in its degree of naturalism and directness. Although the compulsion to fill every square inch of space with design is conspicuous in these carvings, they are quite free of the extreme elaboration that is sometimes adduced as evidence of barbarism in less enlightened styles of Maya art.

4

PIEDRAS NEGRAS, GUATEMALA

The Acropolis

COMPLETE reports on excavations at Piedras Negras by expeditions of the University Museum, University of Pennsylvania, are not yet available, but sections of a projected series have been published recently as PIEDRAS NEGRAS ARCHAEOLOGY: ARCHITECTURE, part 1, no. 1 (1943) and parts 2, 4, and 6 (1944) by Linton Satterthwaite Jr. The Museum's PIEDRAS NEGRAS PRELIMINARY PAPERS, no. 1 (1933) and no. 3 (1935), also describe acropolis buildings. This plate is used here by courtesy of the University Museum.

The back of a throne in Structure J-6 is shown below.

PIEDRAS NEGRAS
The Acropolis

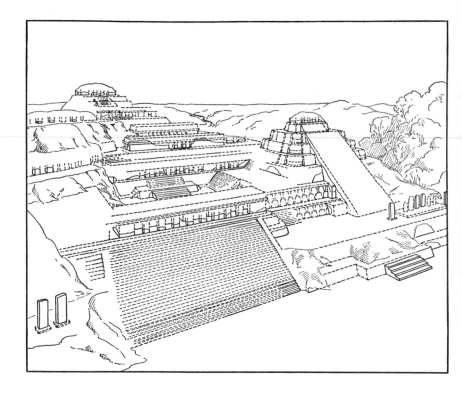

IN ANCIENT times the Usumacinta River was probably a busy artery of trade and travel. Starting at the confluence of the Rio de la Pasion and the Rio Salinas, it now forms the boundary between Chiapas, Mexico, and the southwestern corner of Department of the Peten, Guatemala. In Tabasco it joins the Grijalva River in a huge delta just before it reaches the Gulf of Mexico at the port of Alvaro Obregon. At intervals the Usumacinta breaks into violent rapids, but it is navigable by canoe for the greater part of its course, becoming impassable only at the rapids of San Jose, shortly before it clears the hills of Chiapas and flows into the open coastal plain. About fifteen or twenty miles above these rapids is the ruined city of Piedras Negras, which the expeditions of the Museum of the University of Pennsylvania, under the direction of J. Alden Mason and Linton Satterthwaite Jr., have excavated and studied for many years. Though not of great size, Piedras Negras is remarkable for the number and superb quality of its sculptured monuments. As one should expect in a city that was located on an important trade route, its artistic creations are influenced by many styles, linking it with such distant regions as that of Copan and of northeastern Peten. This eclecticism is reflected in the varied techniques and designs of its stelae, though Piedras Negras sculpture, whether executed in high, three-quarters relief or in bas-relief scarcely raised from its background, maintains an excellence peculiarly its own.

Stone carving at Piedras Negras was never an adjunct of architecture, as it was to a great extent at Copan. Architectural decoration was almost entirely confined to stucco, and the scarcity of the fragments that remain indicates that even such ornament was restrained. Pleasing effects depended upon the refinement of proportions, made possible by technical improvements in the construction of the vault. Thin walls and multiple doorways give this architecture a grace apparently never quite achieved by the more conservative builders of Tikal and other cities of northeastern Peten.

The Acropolis of Piedras Negras is built on a natural hill, the contours of which are modified by a rising series of courts, in part artificially built up by constructions which were consecutively abandoned and covered over with fills of loose rubble. The natural irregularity of the terrain did not encourage a rigidly formal arrangement, but even as the plans were altered and expanded, the builders never lost sight of an obviously deliberate scheme. The principal approach is by a single, broad stairway, flanked by two pyramidal structures and by long platforms supporting rows of stelae. The stairway leads to a building of many doorways, through which one enters an enclosed quadrangle, surrounded by higher terraces and rectangular buildings. Beyond this, two more courts at still higher levels rise to the crest of the composition, a small palace, overlooking the river flowing nearly three hundred feet below. Each court is protected from direct approach by the surrounding buildings, and, in the spaces between them, by light masonry walls with small openings which permit the passage of one person. It was not fear of military attack, however, that motivated such exclusiveness, for many wide stairways and entrances lead to all parts of the Acropolis. It is better explained by a desire to screen the activities inside the courts from the view of the plaza below. The latter was open to the citizens at large, and was used, no doubt, for public ceremonies and gatherings; and access to the Acropolis seems to have been the prerogative of nobles, priests, and neophytes, who performed secret rites, debated issues of state, or pored over abstruse manuscripts in the long palace buildings, safeguarded from the rude approach of the laity.

5

PIEDRAS NEGRAS, GUATEMALA

Structure K-5 3d

PART 1 of "The Evolution of a Maya Temple" by Linton Satterthwaite Jr., published in the UNIVERSITY MUSEUM BULLETIN for November 1939, deals with the early and middle stages of Structure K-5, showing them in isometric projection.

The pottery incense burner is from Structure K-5 and is partly restored.

PIEDRAS NEGRAS
Structure K-5 3d

VAULTED construction does not appear in the earliest periods at Piedras Negras. Possibly builders in the Usumacinta region had already developed an architecture that employed masonry walls roofed with perishable materials at the time when stone-vaulted buildings were gaining popularity in northeastern Peten, and perhaps they were reluctant to sacrifice the room space and wide openings that this type of roofing permitted, for the sake of greater permanence and greater height, at least until the vault had been so improved that it could be adapted to their traditional style. At any rate, Structure K-5 3d (earliest phase of K-5), which is overlaid by two later pyramids, was almost certainly not vaulted. It is a single large room, about eighteen feet wide, a span too great for an early vault and perhaps too great even for a flat roof formed of wooden beams and capped with mortar and stone. Such roofs were probably common at Piedras Negras; but although it is not certain when they first were introduced, they are found usually on buildings which show a strong influence from the Peten. Structure K-5 3d, on the other hand, except for its lower terraces, which are elaborated by inset corners and apron moldings in the Peten manner, is quite unlike other buildings at Piedras Negras and may stem from an earlier tradition. The restoration therefore shows a roof of thatch, which seems the most likely solution, since thatch is even now commonly used on pole constructions and sometimes may be seen also on masonry houses in Guatemala.

The single room of the temple is severely rectangular and, for its entire length, a bench runs against its rear wall. A small cylindrical altar of stone, very slightly greater in diameter at the top, stands in the middle of the room, set into the floor. Another is outside, on the pyramid and immediately before the temple steps, as if outdoor rites were preferred in good weather. Both are stained black, probably by the smoke of copal, a resinous incense that the Maya still employ in their religious ceremonies. Ancient pottery censers attest the antiquity of this custom and present an interesting variety of elaborate and grotesque forms, most often anthropomorphic. The hideous specimen illustrated here is of somewhat later date than Structure K-5 3d, from which we have no examples of sculptural or plastic art, and its crude workmanship is not necessarily an indication of an era of inferior culture but rather of the low caste of its creator, doubtless some obscure craftsman, peddling his wares on the temple steps to all who came to make an offering.

6

PIEDRAS NEGRAS, GUATEMALA

Structure K-5 1st

THE READER is directed to "The Evolution of a Maya Temple," part 2, in the UNIVERSITY MUSEUM BULLETIN for March-May 1940.

The stucco head was probably part of the decoration of the roof comb.

PIEDRAS NEGRAS
Structure K-5 1st

IN TIME, the terraces of K-5 3d gave way at the rear, causing a settling of the temple walls. Its design was then already outmoded by a style that strove for greater height, and the whole pyramid was raised by the addition of two terraces which entirely buried the old temple. Doubtless a new one was constructed on the higher level, but since it was completely torn down at a still later period, we know nothing whatever about its design, though two small altars, in precisely the same position as before, show that ceremonial procedure had not greatly changed. Probably the general plan of the temple also remained the same, for the pyramid in this stage, except for added height, retained its original proportions. The projecting masses at the front and rear were built after the second temple was razed, and served to make room for a building which inaugurated a new style characterized by greater elaboration of plan. Of this building, only the platform and a fragment of wall remain, for it, in turn, was demolished and replaced by another, which is the subject of this plate.

A great many alterations and additions followed each other in this final period, but their exact sequence is doubtful, and it is not altogether certain that all the features depicted in this drawing actually were contemporaneous. The masks decorating the pyramid are later than the terraces behind them, but it is merely an assumption that they were built before the final additions to the temple itself, which are so ruined that they could not be shown. Even the main building walls are standing to a height of only a few feet, and the character of the upper façade must be surmised from the plan alone. However, the presence in the room of fragments of stucco sculpture, such as would be used for the decoration of a roof comb, definitely indicates this feature, and from the dimensions of the large stucco head shown here one can even estimate the size of the human figure that must have formed its central motif.

There seems to be no way to tell how long a period of time is represented by the gradual growth of this structure. There certainly must have been considerable intervals when the successive buildings were in use and when no changes

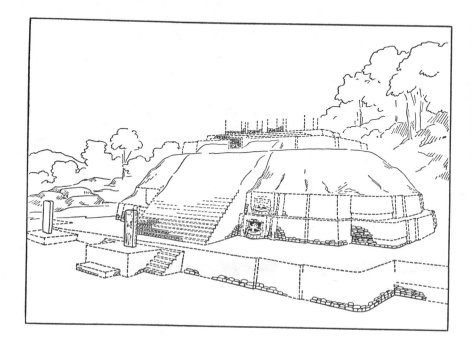

were being made. The stela in front of the main stairway was not set up until after the pyramid had attained substantially its final form, which must have been prior to A.D. 677. The second monument was erected about five years later, and it may be that the sculptured panel on the stairway also bears this date, though its inscription is badly eroded. These dates are very near to the beginning of the great period in Maya art. If we consider the unusual character of the early building, which probably denotes a regional style, we can see how in each successive stage the growing influence of northeastern Peten heralds the consolidation of Old Empire traditions.

7

PIEDRAS NEGRAS, GUATEMALA

A Maya Sweat Bath

THIS BUILDING, known as Structure P-7, is described in AN UNUSUAL TYPE OF BUILDING IN THE MAYA OLD EMPIRE (1936) by Linton Satterthwaite Jr. In MAYA AND MEXICAN SWEAT HOUSES (1938) Frank M. Cresson Jr. establishes the function of Maya sweat houses and describes the customs of ceremonial bathing in ancient and in modern Mexico.

The grotesque head, a leg of Altar 4, may represent a rain god.

PIEDRAS NEGRAS
A Maya Sweat Bath

THE CLEAR-CUT distinction that our civilization attempts to draw between therapeutics and religion did not exist in older cultures. Good health may not have been synonymous with spiritual purity, but healing often implied driving out of the body certain evil influences accessible to both physical and spiritual forces. Ceremonial purification had, therefore, both a medical and a psychological function, and the sweat bath, or more accurately, the steam bath, accompanied by appropriate ceremonies, was admirably suited to perform both. When a man was stricken with disease or when a neophyte was to be initiated into the sacred mysteries, he repaired to the bath, where priests who specialized in the procedure ministered to his needs.

There are no less than eight sweat baths among the ruins at Piedras Negras. They are easily identified by the distinctive contours of their remains, though they vary in size and in degree of elaboration. Structure P-7 is one of the largest and most prominent of these buildings. It contains a low, vaulted chamber in which is a hearth built of stone and lined with potsherds to resist the heat of fire. The entrance to this chamber is very small, and is approached by a sunken passage, which at the same time served as a drain to carry off the water used in the bath. The passage continues inside between two benches, on which the bathers lay, fanning about their bodies with a bundle of leafy twigs the steam which rose from the hot stones of the hearth when water was thrown upon them. The steam chamber is enclosed in a rectangular building divided into two rooms by a medial wall. These were probably used for dressing and for rest, as well as for ceremonies in connection with the cure or purification. The projection of the central chamber into the rear room subdivides this again into two parts, so that the building in effect has four chambers. When Teobert Maler first examined the ruin, he called it the Temple of the Eight Chambers, apparently with the mistaken notion that there were four ranges of rooms. It is easy to see the source of his error in the peculiar roof construction of this building. The sloping face of the vault could be seen, apparently standing to its full height on one side, and if he assumed, as he had every reason to do, that it was capped

with stone slabs, he had to postulate the existence of a wall to uphold the missing side of the vault in about what is actually the middle of the room. It is not surprising that the possibility of resting a beam-and-mortar roof on a corbel did not occur to him, for this is still the only known example in the Maya Old Empire of this ingenious type of construction.

Perhaps because P-7 was to some extent a utilitarian structure, it was decorated very simply, if at all, and there are no traces of stucco or stone ornament. The carved stone head illustrated on the title page of this drawing has no direct connection with the sweat bath, but is one of the four supports of a rectangular altar in the plaza on which the building faces.

8

COPAN, HONDURAS

The Acropolis

A GUIDE BOOK to the ruins of Copan has been prepared by Gustav Strömsvik for publication by the Government of Honduras. Photographs and drawings, made, however, before much excavation had been done, appear in the BIOLOGIA CENTRALI-AMERICANA and in the first volume of the MEMOIRS OF THE PEABODY MUSEUM OF AMERICAN ARCHAEOLOGY AND ETHNOLOGY. THE INSCRIPTIONS AT COPAN (1920) by Sylvanus G. Morley also contains much general information about the site.

The bat is a roof ornament from one of the buildings now destroyed.

COPAN
The Acropolis

FROM THE map one can see that Copan is far to the southeast of the center of the Maya Old Empire. In the country beyond there are no other large cities with vaulted buildings and sculptured monuments. Yet there is about it nothing of the character of a frontier city. There are no fortifications to indicate that its relations with neighbors to the south and east were anything but friendly, and there is little in its art which suggests foreign influences. If anything, the art of Copan surpasses that of the Peten and is strikingly individual, as if the city were itself the nucleus of a cultural subdivision of the Old Empire. In most Peten cities architectural decoration was executed in stucco, and sculpture is largely confined to stelae and altars, whereas at Copan stone carvings, often in full round, adorned every important building.

As if jealous of this superb creation of man, all the most violent forces of nature seem to have conspired to destroy it. Even in historic times, earthquakes have shaken the ruins, and now the beautifully carved fragments of its buildings lie scattered on the slopes of its pyramids like the pieces of a gigantic jigsaw puzzle in stone. The Copan River has wantonly changed its course to gnaw at the east side of the Acropolis. It has devoured entire several buildings and has washed away thousands of tons of stone, leaving exposed a vertical cut a hundred and eighty-five feet in height. Seen thus in section, ancient plaza floors and the remains of partially dismantled walls, covered by layer upon layer of later construction, testify to untold centuries of human effort.

In 1935 the Government of Honduras and the Carnegie Institution of Washington came to the rescue with a joint project to deflect the course of the river, then threatening to consume what remained of the East Court. Mr. Gustav Strömsvik, of the Institution, undertook also to supervise the excavation and restoration of some of the better-preserved structures. Now, after eight seasons' work, the principal group has been partially cleared of debris, and as much as possible of the sculpture has been set back in place, where it is protected from further erosion. Although little remains of superstructures, the visitor can now form some conception of the former magnificence of this old city from the design and ornament of building foundations.

The plan of the Acropolis is formal and typical of the Old Empire Maya. The large rectangular plaza is surrounded by steps from which people could view the ceremonies, and on it are placed the principal monuments, each with its accompanying altar. In the center of the plaza was a small platform, now reduced to a mere mound of stone. Another insignificant mound has been removed and is not shown in the present drawing, since little could be learned about its form and since its unsymmetrical position seems to imply that it was placed there as an afterthought, perhaps even when the city was already falling into ruin. The ball court divides the Main Plaza from the Court of the Hieroglyphic Stairway, which is bounded on the south by a wide flight of steps leading up to Structure 11. Behind this temple are the Reviewing Stand and the East and West Courts, dominated by the high pyramid of Structure 16. Though formal, the arrangement is not rigidly precise. Corners are never exact right angles and conspicuous decorative features are only approximately centered. Probably these imperfections were not intentional and were caused by successive changes, as new and ever more ambitious projects threw out of alignment such older features as were retained. It is, in fact, remarkable that in the course of so many alterations the group as a whole still managed to preserve a very definite scheme of arrangement, which evidences a conscious regard on the part of the ancient builders for the formal composition of group architecture.

Two errors must be noted in the restoration. There should be a rectangular altar (L) behind Stela 2 on the north mound of the ball court. Stela 3, which stands on the main plaza south of the open platform, is wrongly depicted as a small monument, whereas it is in fact comparable in size and form to the other large monuments on the plaza.

9

COPAN, HONDURAS
The Hieroglyphic Stairway

Georck Byron Gordon describes the early excavations undertaken by the Peabody Museum of American Archaeology and Ethnology in The Hieroglyphic Stairway, Ruins of Copan (1902). The inscription is analyzed by Sylvanus G. Morley in The Inscriptions at Copan (1920).

The figure is the lowest of the five that grace the Hieroglyphic Stairway.

COPAN
The Hieroglyphic Stairway

ONE OF THE spectacular structures that justify the fame of Copan is Structure 26, which adjoins the east building of the ball court and juts out northward from the mass of the upper Acropolis courts. It is a high, stepped pyramid on which once stood a temple now entirely destroyed. Its former ornateness can be judged only by scattered bits of sculpture and by the grandiose stairway which formed its approach on the west. Almost every stone of this stairway is covered with carving. The steep ramps at the sides are decorated with a design of conventionalized serpent-head and bird motifs, each riser of the steps is inscribed with a row of hieroglyphs, and heroic seated statues are placed at intervals on the central axis.

When John G. Owens of the Peabody Museum first began his excavations on the stairway, little was to be seen on the surface but a mass of fallen sculpture and a section comprising fifteen consecutive steps, which appeared to be in position. After digging was begun, however, it became clear that this series of steps had slipped downward for a considerable distance, as if it had been dislodged by the sudden shock of an earthquake, and that, as found, it actually overlapped the base of the stairway, which still remained intact beneath it. This extraordinary accident was made possible by the steepness of the stairway, a very common trait of such Maya structures, in which the treads of the steps actually measure less than the risers, reversing the proportion usual in modern design. Before excavation was well under way, Mr. Owens died at Copan of one of those malignant fevers that are a dreaded hazard to all travelers in Middle America, but his work was continued by his former assistant, who later published a detailed report. The repair of the stairway was one of the chief projects of the cooperative undertaking of the Government of Honduras and the Carnegie Institution of Washington, and was completed in 1942.

Much of the restoration is of necessity tentative and conjectural, although the general arrangement is clear from the standing lower portion. A large part of the inscription, however, could be put together only on the basis of an assumed chronological sequence of dates, and many of the stones had to be replaced at random. Even the spacing of the central figures is somewhat doubtful.

It is regrettable that we do not know the character of the events recorded in this long inscription. Since much of it consists of calendrical dates which are all within the known time-span of the city's prosperity, it may recount the history

of Copan and the exploits of its rulers. On the other hand, it is more likely that it is a record of astronomical observations, perpetuated in stone in order to serve as a base for future calculations and prophesies. The dates run from about A.D. 540 to 746. It is Dr. Morley's opinion, based chiefly on the arrangement of the dates but consistent also with the style of sculpture, that the construction of the stairway was begun, or at least projected, about 710, and that it was finally completed and formally dedicated in 756 by the erection of Stela M at its base.

10
COPAN, HONDURAS
The Ball Court

A FULL REPORT on excavations conducted by the Carnegie Institution of Washington on this and other structures at Copan is not yet available. For a general description of Maya ball courts and the game see THE MAYA BALL GAME POK-TA-POK (1932) by Frans Blom.

The ball-court marker is from the middle court.

COPAN
The Ball Court

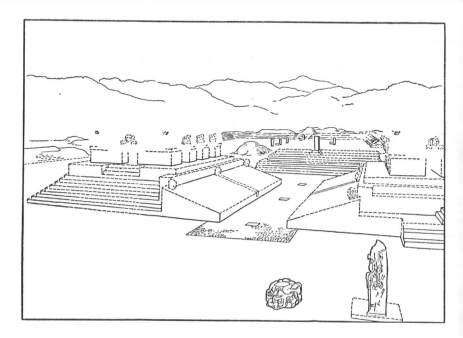

WE ARE so accustomed to impute to ancient peoples a sort of pompous religiosity that sometimes their activities seem to us to have been an endless round of ceremonial gestures which had no purpose beyond the self-hypnotic awe that they inspired. It is refreshing to turn to a more frivolous aspect of their life and learn that the Aztec and the Maya both appreciated a good ball game as much as does any modern enthusiast. Even if the ritual which so pervaded their activities also played a part in their games, it made them in no way less sporting. Duran, having observed the games in Mexico, writes that, "A great multitude of nobles and gentlemen took part, and they played with such content and joy, changing now some and later others . . . and so content that the sun would go down before they knew it." There were also professional players, and the pious Spanish friars were shocked by the heavy bets that were sometimes laid on their success. The Maya were in all things more restrained than the barbarous Aztec and probably less often gambled away their livelihood, but there is no reason to suppose that their games were more solemn or less exciting. Their courts resembled in plan those of Mexico, and though the playing rules must have differed in detail, we can get a general idea of the Maya game from reading Mexican accounts.

The ball was of solid rubber, sometimes as much as a foot in diameter. It was passed between teams ranged on opposite ends of the court, and the players could hit it only with their knees or their hips, points being scored when the opponents failed to return it correctly. In central Mexico, and in late times in Yucatan, rings of stone were set high up in the side walls of the court, and it was considered a particular triumph for a player to knock the ball through the ring. It is said that on such occasions the spectators forfeited the very garments they wore to the lucky player, and that a general stampede usually ensued. Perhaps Maya custom never stooped to such indignity; at any rate we find no stone rings on the older Maya courts, although the carved markers may have served in some way as special objectives.

Maya ball players wore for protection a pad on the knee, a quilted arm-guard, and a sort of skirt or apron of leather over the hips. Serious accidents, however, must have been frequent, for the solid ball was heavy, and the game as described was swift and strenuous.

Particularly skillful players were held in high repute, and the game itself, even in Old Empire times, must have been an ancient and highly honored institution. Every town of any importance had at least one ball court, and sometimes several, constructed of stone and placed prominently among important civic and religious buildings. Under the flagged paving of the latest court of Copan, which was built probably about A.D. 775, excavation revealed two earlier courts, the lowest of which is about three and a half feet below the present level of the plaza and, unlike the others, has markers of stucco. Evidently the Maya considered recreation to be as essential in their civic life as their more sedate pageants and sacrifices, for from the first, the ball court was an integral part of the plan of the Acropolis, and through all its alterations it maintained a place of conspicuous importance.

11
COPAN, HONDURAS
The Jaguar Stairway

THE JAGUAR STAIRWAY is mentioned in the first volume of the BIOLOGIA CENTRALI-AMERICANA, Archaeology (1889-1902) by A. P. Maudslay, and in PREHISTORIC RUINS OF COPAN, HONDURAS, volume I of the MEMOIRS OF THE PEABODY MUSEUM OF AMERICAN ARCHAEOLOGY AND ETHNOLOGY (1896). Both are early accounts, written before thorough excavation was made. TEMPLE XXII AT COPAN (1939) by Aubrey S. Trik is a complete report on that structure.

The head of the young corn god fell from the upper zone of Structure 22.

COPAN
The Jaguar Stairway

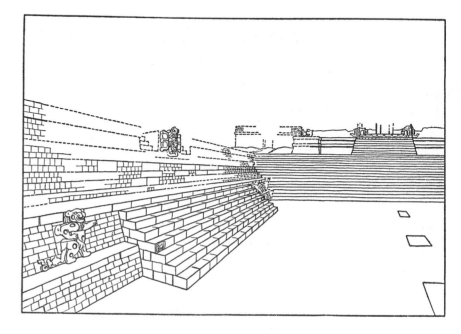

THE SNAKE and jaguar figure prominently in Maya mythology and were often represented in painting and in sculpture. The artistic treatment of the two, however, is strikingly different. The serpent, for the most part, was conventionalized almost beyond recognition, as if his supernatural powers freed him of the compulsion to restrict himself to his earthly form. The jaguar, on the other hand, remained a relatively normal animal whenever he was depicted. The two guardians of the stairway which leads down into the East Court at Copan, with their rampant postures and snarling mouths, are forthright representations of the dreaded beast of the forest. Their collars and loincloths, and the bright red paint on their bodies, gleaming with spots of inlay, are their only concessions to the decorum of civilization. In contrast, the central motif is purely symbolic. Held in the mouth of the serpent creature is the anthropomorphic head of the sun god, recognized by his huge square eyes, the fillet that passes beneath them with a twist over the nose, and his characteristically filed incisors. On each side are motifs which suggest the hieroglyph for the planet Venus. The cycle of Venus is correlated in one of the Maya codices with the cycle of the solar year, and it is not unlikely that this carving expresses the myth connected with these phenomena. Three carved rectangular slabs set into floor of the East Court are centered on the stairway and apparently are part of its composition. They are so eroded, however, that the subject of the carving can no longer be made out.

On Structure 22, in the background, is another example of the serpent, whose open mouth here forms the principal doorway to the temple. Only the lower part of his jaw, with curved fangs and molars which are sculptured in the form of bird heads, is still in place, but if the skeptical readers doubts the identification, he can easily trace the development of this ubiquitous motif through its more naturalistic aspects. Serpent-mouth doorways are not reported from the Peten, but are characteristic of a style to the north, in the region known as the Chenes, and as far south as Rio Bec in southern Campeche. At one time there must have been direct communication between these regions and Copan, probably by coastal or sea trade routes that bypassed the cities of the Peten. If the serpent-mouth motif was imported at Copan, it was nevertheless transformed by the skill of the native architects and combined with other more naturalistic forms. The so-called "singing girls" of Copan, more probably portraits of the youthful corn god or his acolytes, were carved in full round. In cross-legged sitting posture they formed part of the façade's design, and together with the great serpent-mouth doorway and the masks on the corners of the building, they embellished the façade of Structure 22 in a manner peculiarly distinctive of Copan.

12

COPAN, HONDURAS

The Reviewing Stand

SYLVANUS G. MORLEY gives a description of the Reviewing Stand, which at that time, however, had not been thoroughly excavated, in THE INSCRIPTIONS AT COPAN (1920).

The head is that of a torchbearer on the Reviewing Stand.

COPAN
The Reviewing Stand

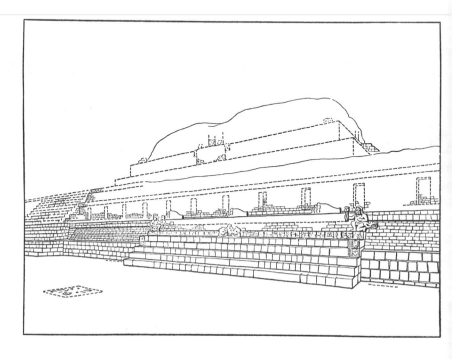

THE DESIGN of the Reviewing Stand parallels so strikingly that of the Jaguar Stairway, and its relation to the West Court is so much like that of the Jaguar Stairway to the East Court, that we can scarcely avoid the conclusion that both had more than a merely decorative function, and were probably adapted to the requirements of some prescribed formal procedure or ceremony. Instead of the two jaguars of the East Court, there are here two crouching human figures, each holding a flaming torch. Their faces are quite un-Maya, and snakes issuing from the corners of their mouths add to their expression of ferocity and create the impression that they are little less savage than the rampant jaguars. Here, too, there is a central motif representing the bust of a man or god, supporting on his shoulders the halves of a large bivalve shell, which recall the Venus symbols of the other composition. The analogy is made complete by three carved slabs, which were found in the West Court, and which probably were set in the floor and centered on the Reviewing Stand, forming a unit of composition in the same way as the sculptured slabs of the East Court do with the Jaguar Stairway. The Reviewing Stand was so named because it is not primarily a means of access to the terraces above, since its highest step does not reach the top of the lowest terrace. Its position overlooking the West Court suggests that it might have served as a grandstand from which high functionaries could conveniently view or direct a ceremony. The Jaguar Stairway was evidently used in like manner, with the open platform behind it perhaps providing standing room for less distinguished observers.

Behind and above the Reviewing Stand is a terrace wall, elaborated by a row of niches, two of which also serve as entrances to a small chamber. In front of the niches lie three colossal conch shells carved in stone. The high mass of the substructure of Structure 11 towers above in a mounting series of terraces. The temple itself is so ruined that not a stone of its façade remains in place. It appears to be an almost solid mass of masonry, crossed by two perpendicular passages, which form the only room space in the building. Its especially massive construction and two interior stairways leading up from the longitudinal passage hint at a second story, of which, however, there are no actual traces. In this drawing, a second story has been restored, whereas in the general view of the Acropolis the possibility is considered that the interior stairways led up to an open roof. From the carved stones scattered on the slopes of the mound, one

can infer that the building was sumptuously decorated. Among the fragments recovered were parts of gigantic standing human figures, and large heads of creatures resembling huge lizards or alligators. Curved fangs and other characteristic fragments show that the north and south doorways simulated the yawning mouths of serpents, as did the entrance to Structure 22.

The Reviewing Stand is not centered on the temple above it, and is probably an earlier feature, for had it been built after the temple or at the same time, there seems to be no reason why it should not have been symmetrically placed. The temple, on the other hand, faces north, and its position is determined by its relation to the composition of the Main Plaza. The inscriptions are not decisive, but tend to confirm this view. The Reviewing Stand was probably dedicated in A.D. 771, and although the date of the erection of Structure 11 is unknown, among the dates inscribed on the jambs of its doorways is one which falls in 773, referring apparently to some event which took place two years after the Reviewing Stand was completed.

13
XPUHIL, CAMPECHE
Structure 1

THE ORIGINAL account of this building appeared in ARCHAEOLOGICAL RECONNAISSANCE IN CAMPECHE, QUINTANA ROO, AND PETEN (1943) by Karl Ruppert and John H. Denison Jr.

The mask is part of a panel flanking one of the door-ways of Structure 1.

XPUHIL
Structure 1

NORTH of the Peten, the tall forests stretch far into Campeche and Quintana Roo, concealing under their dense vegetation innumerable ruins that no one yet has visited or mapped. Oddly enough, it is to the gum-chewing habit of our sedentary city-dwellers that we owe what little knowledge we have of the mysteries hidden in this deserted land, for the only people who frequent it now are the hardy chicleros who roam the forests in search of the sapodilla trees from which they gather sap for the manufacture of chewing gum. Often they come upon artificial mounds, worked stones, fragments of sculpture, and here and there the walls of some ruined building scarcely visible through the thick masses of foliage. It is they who guide the archaeologist over the narrow, overgrown trails, for they alone know where the ruins are, and where to find adequate sources of water to carry on the difficult journey from day to day.

The southernmost sites of Campeche are similar to those of the Peten, but as one travels northward one encounters more and more often sites which have a distinctive style of architecture in sharp contrast to that of the south. This style is designated as Rio Bec, after one of its southernmost sites, or sometimes as Rio Bec–Chenes to include also the architecture of northern Campeche, which is merely a variant of the same style. It is characterized by lavish ornament not only of the upper zone, but also of the lower walls of the buildings. Important doorways are usually flanked by highly conventionalized heads of serpents in profile, whose open jaws form the entrance. Above them, large masks with prominently protruding teeth completely cover the upper zone, breaking through and displacing the medial molding. Two solid towers of masonry, which resemble in form the pyramid temples of the Peten, are often the most striking feature of such a building. Structure 1 at Xpuhil is even more than ordinarily pretentious, and has three such towers, ascended by stairways that incline only twenty degrees from the vertical, and hardly could have been designed for actual use. In fact, another stair of more normal proportions leads from the terrace of the building, through the south tower, and to the level of the roof. One can think of no practical object served by these towers other than to evade the limitations imposed by a rigid habit of construction which did not permit buildings of more than one story. The solid decorative masses not only achieve an imposing effect by their height, but also break the severely rectangular contour of the building and produce an interesting silhouette. Their sophisticated simulation of functional forms marks the style as derivative, though no earlier examples from which one could draw a direct line of evolution are known, and its origin still awaits further efforts of research and discovery. Since there are no sculptured monuments directly associated with Rio Bec buildings, it is impossible to assign a date to these constructions without stratigraphic studies. We can only infer from the uniformity of their highly stylized decoration that the examples we know belong to the same general period, most probably roughly contemporaneous with late Old Empire times.

SAYIL, YUCATAN

The Palace

FOR DRAWINGS and photographs of this structure see the monographs issued in 1928 by the Ministry of Public Education of Mexico, mentioned on page xii of the introduction.

The serpent is part of the "diving god" motif on the second story of the palace.

SAYIL
The Palace

THE FLAT limestone plain of northern Yucatan is broken by a range of hills that starts near Campeche on the west coast of the peninsula, runs northeastward, and then turns to the southeast, forming an angle with its apex to the north. In the region defined by this angle, named the Puuc from the Maya word for hills, was developed a style of architecture conspicuous for its careful workmanship in stone. Facing stones are accurately squared, smoothly finished, and nicely fitted together. In section they are very thin, forming a veneer that adheres to the surface of the wall, the body of which is a monolithic mass of rubble and mortar. This technique of building is not limited to the Puuc region, but here, after a long development, it attained a consummate refinement. Decoration tends to be elaborate, but more abstract and geometric than the naturalistic sculpture of Copan, where each motif is an individual masterpiece. Puuc sculpture is something in the nature of a mosaic, formed of separately carved elements fitted together in a variety of motifs. The elements themselves, however, are for the most part standardized forms, and were probably produced in quantity by minor craftsmen for the use of the architect. Masks, applied colonnettes, spools, stepped frets, and X-shaped units set together to produce crosshatching are the main elements of decoration, whereas human figures and other naturalistic forms play a minor role and, where used, are more often executed in stucco.

The Puuc style is the culmination of centuries of slow progress, and many buildings in the same area show the cruder workmanship and simpler ornament of earlier periods. The oldest unit of the palace at Sayil is undecorated save for a simple rectangular molding on its principal façade. At one time this unit was an independent structure, and it was never remodeled but simply incorporated in the first story of the palace when the stairway was built, and another, more ornate, wing added to the east of it. The resulting lack of symmetry is not offensive to the eye, however, for the wings are not parallel. Each recedes slightly from the stairway, and the two can be viewed together only from a considerable distance, when their differences in detail become inconspicuous. Attention is centered on the second story, which is one of the most successful examples of its type. The columned doorways are a common feature in Yucatan, and their rhythmic alteration with simple rectangular

openings is one of the pleasing traits of the Puuc style. On the upper zone, the rhythm finds an echo in the alteration of the ubiquitous mask motif with a less formal design consisting of a "diving god," a grotesque upsidedown creature between two abbreviated serpents.

The technique and arrangement of the ornament on the third story is very different. Large sections of the façade are left plain, and above each doorway an isolated ornament of stucco has crumbled away, exposing rough tenons projecting from the masonry. To judge from the arrangement of these tenons it seems probable that they once supported human figures, and that the design projected above the level of the roof to break its simple silhouette. In spite of the difference in decorative technique, there is no indication that the third story was built much later than the second, and it is clear that the former was part of the original plan, for no rooms are superimposed and each higher story rests on a block of solid masonry designed for its support. This forthright simplicity of arrangement, combined with a casual disregard of minor imperfections of symmetry and a freedom from the oppressively monotonous intricacy of ornament that mars many Puuc structures, makes the Sayil palace one of the most satisfactory compositions that the Maya ever created.

15

LABNA, YUCATAN

The Palace

SEE MONOGRAPHS issued in 1928 by the Ministry of Public Education of Mexico, mentioned on page xii of the introduction.

The incomplete mask is from the upper zone of the east wing.

LABNA
The Palace

IN MANY ways this structure is a characteristic example of Puuc architecture. The masks, the colonnettes applied both to the upper and the lower zones of the façade, the small cylindrical drums that decorate the lower member of the moldings and the plinth, the two-column doorways, all are typical of the style. The only dramatic and original feature is the grotesque mask that leers from the corner of the east wing. Although it somewhat resembles the usual Maya serpent, it has lost all correspondence with natural form. As a focus of interest in the design, the curious subject attracts less attention than the intricate pattern of shadows cast by its strongly projecting elements and successfully relieving the monotony of the repeated standard motifs.

On a lower level at the left is a simpler building in the early Puuc style. The rectangular molding is shown in the restoration as rising over the doorway, but this is an error. It does rise over all other doorways in the building, but for some reason, this entrance is the exception and here the molding runs straight across as is shown in the sketch. Possibly no entrance was planned here originally, for the room has another doorway which later was blocked with masonry, and the apparent inconsistency may be due to a change in plan occasioned by the building of the palace foundations which abut upon the earlier walls.

The second story is made up of several discrete structures. The building shown in the drawing is now little more than a formless mound of debris, but its restoration is based on analogy with a building of similar plan, placed symmetrically with respect to the central axis of the palace and still standing almost to the full height of its upper zone.

In spite of some attempt at balance and symmetry, the Labna palace, especially when compared with that of Sayil, seems to lack unity and compactness, perhaps because, like many Maya structures, it was not built according to a preconceived plan, but grew by accretion as the exigencies of changing times demanded. The first story was originally a group of separate buildings, later

tied together by the platform upholding the second story. This platform, in fact, was never completed, nor was the east wing, and at the back, where the two join, one can still see open fill supported only by rough retaining walls. Building operations in ancient times required much labor, which was available only during the rainless months when farming activities were at a standstill. Many years were required for the completion of a single large structure, and with repeated alterations, expansions, and changes of plan, building must have been going on continuously in the larger Maya cities. When it finally ceased, many large projects were left unfinished, as if the source of effort that went into their construction did not dwindle gradually but was arrested in midstream by something momentous and unforeseen.

16
LABNA, YUCATAN
The Portal Vault

SEE MONOGRAPHS issued in 1928 by the Ministry
of Public Education of Mexico, mentioned on page xii
of the introduction.

*The sculptured panel is from the lower zone of the east
range of Structure 11.*

LABNA

The Portal Vault

About two hundred yards south of the palace at Labna, and connected with it by a paved roadway, is another cluster of buildings, dominated by a high pyramid temple. A typical Puuc feature of this group is the imposing archway which leads into a rectangular court surrounded by buildings of the "palace" type. Commonly such an archway is an integral part of a palace and is centered on its principal façade, but less frequently, an independent arch serves as a monumental gateway. The Labna portal seems to be a fusion of the two types. Functionally it resembles the former, but instead of being incorporated in a palace building, it is in itself a complete unit, and its two diminutive rooms are definitely subordinate to the large entrance which is the hub of the design.

Standard stone elements are combined with stucco in the decoration of this portal. On each side of the upper zone is a representation of a thatch-roofed house executed in stone, while a tenon projecting from the back wall and the traces of green featherwork of a headdress indicate that originally there was a stucco figure in the doorway, sitting cross-legged as the Maya do. There are other small tenons to carry stucco ornament flanking the archway.

Little now remains of the roof comb which crowned the composition. About all one can infer from the few courses of stone in position is that it was built in three separate units, and had small rectangular openings. At least two distinct types of roof combs occur in the Puuc. One type depends for decorative effect on perforated stonework frequently in the form of a fret motif, and is clearly divided into horizontal zones by three-member moldings, consisting of a rectangular course of small stones between two beveled courses. The other has only simple rectangular windows, and if there is a stone molding, it also is plain and rectangular. Such roof combs invariably carry stucco decoration. The stepped triangular silhouette restored here is rare, and is reported only from the architecture of the east coast and from two buildings at Uxmal. It is definitely suggested, however, by the three-fold division of the roof comb as well as by the arrangement of its windows.

On the left is a building which demonstrates the occasional tendency of Puuc architecture to fall back on mere surface ornament to relieve the severity of a simple mass. The pattern is a solid area of sculpture, meaningless as a kaleidoscopic design which results automatically from elementary principles of symmetry. It reveals the poverty of inspiration of an affluent age which is already replete with traditional motifs and has little more to offer in the way of original design. The trifling value placed on the craft of carving is reflected in the lavish and casual use of sculptured elements arranged with little aesthetic significance, and serving simply to create the effect of a prodigally rich texture.

17
KABAH, YUCATAN
Palace Group

SEE MONOGRAPHS issued in 1928 by the Ministry of Public Education of Mexico, mentioned on page xii of the introduction.

The mask forms a step in an interior doorway of the Codz Poop.

KABAH

Palace Group

THE TENDENCY to rely for effect on surface decoration culminated finally in an indiscriminate piling-up of ornament and the elimination of all plain surfaces. The façade of Structure 1 at Kabah, locally known as the Codz Poop, is made up entirely of identical sculptured masks placed side by side and tier upon tier so that the separate motifs merge into a single intricate pattern of shades and deep shadows. In view of the tremendous amount of skilled labor involved in carving so many individual pieces of stone, the artistic effect achieved is disappointing, and one regrets that the originality of the designer was not equal to the craftsmanship of the artisan. The highly cultured and pious aristocracy of the Maya Old Empire would have scorned such baroque ostentation, the product of a later, more secular, civilization seeking to impress the populace with a spectacular display of technical skill. There is some indication that the building was designed to have two stories, for its inner core is a solid mass of masonry, though no stairway is provided for. Perhaps the builders themselves were discouraged by the results of their efforts by the time the mask façade was completed, and terminated the extravagance by substituting a simple roof comb for the intended second story. This change of plan may be in a measure responsible for the ineffectual pretensions of this building which was obviously meant to dominate the composition of the group. Certainly in its present form it fails to score against the rhythmic simplicity of the classic Puuc tradition expressed in Structure 2, the two-story palace seen in the background, which is more severe, more restful, and more consistent in its design.

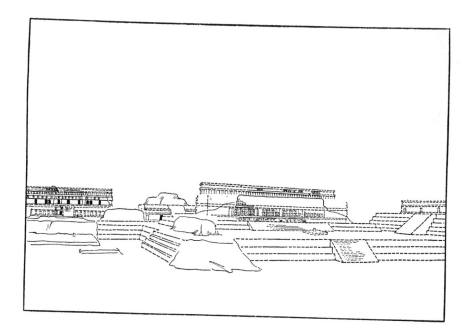

18

UXMAL, YUCATAN
The Monjas Quadrangle

SEE MONOGRAPHS issued in 1928 by the Ministry of Public Education of Mexico, mentioned on page xii of the introduction, and for a general description of the city, "Ancient Temples and Cities of the New World: Uxmal, the city of the Xius," by Sylvanus G. Morley in the BULLETIN OF THE PAN AMERICAN UNION for April 1911.

The sculptured motif is from the east range.

UXMAL
The Monjas Quadrangle

THE ARCHITECTURE of the Puuc is remarkably uniform, as if this region had been closely united and had enjoyed relative isolation from adjacent areas. Uxmal is the only large city which seems to be cosmopolitan in character and shows influences from the Chenes region as well as a touch of the Mexican style that probably at a later time flowered at Chichen Itza. Predominantly, however, it preserves the Puuc traditions. The thatch-roofed house that formed the principal motif of the Portal Vault at Labna is duplicated on the south and north ranges of the quadrangle known as the Monjas or Nunnery. The masks, the crosshatching, the small cylindrical drums decorating the plinth of the walls, are all characteristic Puuc details. Southern traits crop up sporadically, as in the design of the high Temple of the Dwarf or of the Magician, better known by its Spanish name as the Adivino. Its upper temple is a Puuc building, but the serpent-mouth doorway just below it is an adaptation from the same motif found in the Chenes region. Excavations have revealed that another structure built in purely Puuc style is buried in the core of the pyramid, so that the Chenes motif appears to be merely a foreign intrusion in a continuous development.

Northern Yucatan was densely populated even at the time of the Spanish conquest, and some of its ancient history has come down to us in the Books of Chilam Balam. These sacred records of the Maya priests include prophesies, rituals, and myths interspersed with brief chronicles and historical allusions. They were compiled in the seventeenth and eighteenth centuries, and were written in the Maya language but in European script. Doubtless in part they were copied from earlier hieroglyphic manuscripts. Uxmal is often mentioned in these documents as one of the members of the Mayapan League, a confederacy of three powerful cities that at one time ruled over northern Yucatan. After the destruction of Chichen Itza, Mayapan rose in power and continued to rule alone until a revolt in which Uxmal participated led to its downfall and abandonment. Unfortunately, the accounts of these dramatic events are sometimes obscure and inconsistent. So far it has proved difficult to correlate them with archaeological finds. It is even hard to understand how three cities so

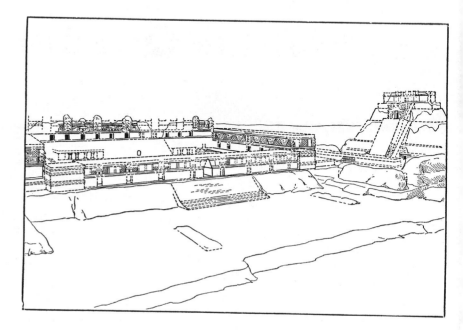

different in architectural style as were Uxmal, Chichen Itza, and Mayapan could have been linked so closely in political association. Uxmal particularly remains an enigma, for although the names of its reputed founders appear to have been Mexican, the ruins of the city are predominantly Maya, with very few traits that could be ascribed to Mexican influence. Therefore, even if Uxmal played an important rôle in the later history of Yucatan, in which the protagonists were Mexican intruders, it seems probable that the period of its greatest prosperity, when its most important buildings were being erected, was far in the past beyond the range of recorded history. Only detailed and comprehensive archaeological studies can reconcile the contradictions, or clarify the incoherent recollections of the Maya historians, who were probably themselves puzzled by the fusion of various traditions current during the final era of Maya civilization.

19

UXMAL, YUCATAN

The Palace of the Governors

SEE MONOGRAPHS issued in 1928 by the Ministry
of Public Education of Mexico, mentioned on page xii
of the introduction.

*The serpent head was found near the Adivino at Uxmal
and is now in the National Museum in Mexico City.*

UXMAL

The Palace of the Governors

THE DESCENDANTS of the ancient family of the Xius still live in villages of northern Yucatan. In their humble circumstances the traditions of their nobility are all but forgotten, and their present mode of life is indistinguishable from that of other Maya Indians whose activities center about the small cornfields that yield them only the bare necessities of life. Formerly, the family commanded honor and prestige, and it is believed that their leader Tutul Xiu founded the city of Uxmal, which for centuries enjoyed hegemony over a large and prosperous district. After the wars with Mayapan, which ended with the razing of that city, the Xius did not return to their original home, but settled at Mani, where the Spaniards found them living in thatch-roofed houses and still warring sporadically with their neighbors. It is claimed that before the conflict, the Palace of the Governors at Uxmal was the residence of their ruler. This may well have been true, though one may question that it was built originally for that purpose, for it is almost too formally designed to make comfortable living quarters even for so august a personage. In any case, it was the most important civic building at Uxmal, and stands on a high, broad, and open platform, overlooking the entire city.

Its style is Puuc, in its most refined and highly developed phase. The veneer stones of its walls are so perfectly fitted that the joints are almost imperceptible, and the carving of its upper zone is a masterpiece of precision and craftsmanship. The problem of decorating this frieze, an uninterrupted area eleven and a half feet high and about three hundred and twenty feet long, was solved in typically Maya fashion by filling it solidly with ornament, which presents a rhythmic repetition of standard elements, accented here and there by the insertion of less conventional figures, and culminating in a central motif, more striking and elaborate than the others. The concentration of ornament in a single large area is not an uncommon trait of Maya buildings, but in justice to the designers it must be noted that this effect is likely to be overemphasized in restoration. The terraces of the Governors' Palace have not been excavated, and one can see only small areas of the retaining walls, where the debris does not cover them altogether. The stonework of these walls is less finished than that of the building, and it is highly probable that there was originally some

stucco design to break the sharp contrast between their severity and the richness of the frieze above.

Moreover, in its original form, the building had two high archways that reached almost to the coping of the roof, piercing the recessed portions, and dividing the composition more sharply into three distinct masses. At a later period, these archways were filled by walls, and the openings were reduced to low doorways. Why this was done it is difficult to understand. The arches are still in perfect condition and the purpose could not have been to bolster a failing construction. It seems hardly more credible, however, that builders would sacrifice such a pleasing aesthetic effect merely for the sake of the small additional room space created. We can ascribe it only to one of those inscrutable vagaries of the Maya mind, which at times baffle the conscientious archaeologist who tries to apprehend their motives.

20

UXMAL, YUCATAN
The Palomas Group

THIS BUILDING and the others shown on the plate are described in "A Group of Related Structures at Uxmal, Mexico" (1910) by Sylvanus G. Morley in the AMERICAN JOURNAL OF ARCHAEOLOGY, second series, volume 14, number 1.

The mask is from the great pyramid to the east of the Palomas group.

UXMAL
Palomas Group

ABUTTING the southwest corner of the terrace on which stands the Governors' Palace is a large pyramid of unusual design. Instead of supporting a temple, its uppermost terrace has rooms on all sides, and is decorated with sculptured stone masks in the manner of a palace building. Above it, on the summit of the pyramid, is a large square platform, apparently open and carrying no constructions at all. This pyramid overlooks to the west a badly ruined group of buildings, which has not yet been excavated or studied thoroughly. Partial clearing of the bush makes it possible to get an idea of the general layout of the buildings, but it is more difficult to apprehend the nature of the individual structures, for what remains of them is covered by deep piles of debris. Two buildings flanking the rear structure of the group were so completely demolished that from surface observation nothing whatever could be learned about them, and they have been left unrestored in the drawing. The façades of other buildings have collapsed almost entirely, and plans are reconstructed mostly from what can be seen of the medial walls, rear walls, and transverse partitions. The decorative treatment is not known in any case except that of the west range of the middle court, which is typically Puuc in character. Nowhere else are sculptured elements in evidence on the surface, and it seems likely that if the upper zones were not plain, as they are reconstructed, only stucco ornament was used.

One of the reasons for including this tentative and incomplete restoration in the series is that it illustrates, better perhaps than others, the fundamental unity of Maya architectural traditions. It at once recalls the design of the Acropolis at Piedras Negras—the same scheme of rectangular courts entirely surrounded by long palace buildings, rising by successive stages to the towering temple which is the focal point of the composition. Local differences are apparent in specific features and specialized decorative techniques. The portal vault and the manner of building stairways with a passageway to permit entrance to the rooms behind it are characteristic of Yucatan, but the basic plan expresses a common intention that clearly attests the uniformity throughout the Maya area not only of building practices, but of the religious and social ends which the buildings served.

Over the medial wall of the forward range of rooms rises the serrated roof comb which suggested to Stephens the form of a dovecote and prompted him to call the structure "The House of the Pigeons," now usually translated into Spanish as Las Palomas. When we consider how few roof combs remain standing above the few first courses of stone, the preservation of this particular structure in a group otherwise so completely in ruin seems almost miraculous. Even bits of decorative stucco still adhere in places to the stone framework, and here and there traces of color can be made out. The design, of course, is obliterated, but the arrangement of projecting tenons indicates a figure or some other dominant motif in the center of each of the stepped triangular units. Roof combs of this type are not reported elsewhere in the Puuc region and are better known as features of the architecture of the east coast of Yucatan, but the chances of finding other examples intact are so slight that it would be unwise to conclude that that of the Palomas was unique or even unusual in the western area. It is very unlikely that the Maya should fail to appreciate the charm that the broken silhouette of such a roof comb could add to the otherwise severely rectangular lines of their buildings.

21

CHICHEN ITZA, YUCATAN

View from the North

BOTH the Government of Mexico and the Carnegie Institution of Washington have carried on excavations and made intensive archaeological studies at Chichen Itza. Many buildings have been partially repaired and the principal groups are being kept clear of vegetation to prevent their further ruin and to permit them to be freely viewed by visitors.

The serpent column is from the doorway of the Temple of the Tigers.

CHICHEN ITZA
View from the North

Centuries after the temples of Chichen Itza were abandoned, pilgrims still came to cast human victims and offerings of gold and jade into the waters of its Sacred Cenote in propitiation of their gods. The fame of the ancient city and its reputed Itza founders was kept alive in song and legend, and the later chronicles of the Maya tell a confused story of its turbulent history. It is not clear whether the Itza were indeed the original founders of the city, which in its early days was purely Maya and closely related in art and architecture to the cities of the Puuc, or whether they were the foreigners who came later, bringing the Mexican traits that distinguished its last great period. Perhaps they were both, for it is said that at one time they abandoned the city and settled at Chakanputun, or Champoton, only to return several centuries later to occupy it again and to rule, together with Mayapan and Uxmal, over the territory of northern Yucatan.

If this was the case, they must have come into close contact during their absence with peoples from central Mexico, perhaps emigrés from the region around Tula, Hidalgo, where recently remains have been discovered that show striking similarities to those of Chichen Itza. Tula is believed to have been the seat of the Toltec who were the precursors of the Aztec in Mexico, and who were devoted to the worship of Quetzalcoatl, a deified culture hero whose symbol was the feathered serpent, as his name implies. In Maya he is called Kukulcan, and his image can be recognized in many sculptures at Chichen Itza, particularly in the serpent columns that embellish the doorways of its pyramid temples. The introduction of this new religious cult and the artistic inspiration of a new style of art and architecture were coincident with a vast social change, of which they were merely the ritual and artistic expressions. The peaceful, sedate, and highly intellectual Maya civilization was a thing of the past. The new culture maintained itself less by tradition than by force of arms. It was dominated by military organization, and was given to exaggerated expressions of brutality and violence. So much at least is reflected in the changed tenor of art, in the decadence of subtle and sensitive modes of expression in favor of ones more crudely literal: wall paintings portray scenes of human sacrifice and of battle, and paucity of hieroglyphic inscriptions indicates waning interest in the astronomical sciences.

However, while the life of the community seems to have declined to a lower, more barbaric plane, the practical art of building was given a new impetus. The span of the vault was increased and it was further adapted to the need for greater interior space by the construction of several parallel vaults supported by long colonnades. Pyramid temples, by their very nature, were restricted to rigidly conventional forms, but civic buildings in plan as well as in assemblage show a new aspiration toward spaciousness. The main group of Chichen Itza is not an acropolis but a broad open plaza, with the Castillo, or, more properly, the Temple of Kukulcan, towering in the center. To the north, a paved roadway leads to the sacred well, whose dark depths hide countless offerings and human sacrifices. To the east is the Group of the Thousand Columns, a large rectangular plaza surrounded by temples and colonnades, once probably a busy marketplace, and to the west, a tremendous ball court, larger than any built before. The buildings are widely separated on a broad level terrace, and beyond the terrace other groups are scattered over a flat, unbounded area. In the background one can see parts of the older city, incorporated with the new, and outlying groups, still covered with tangled vegetation, lie concealed in the monotonous expanse of bush that stretches to the horizon.

22

CHICHEN ITZA, YUCATAN

The Monjas

A DETAILED REPORT on the excavations in the Monjas group is being prepared for the Carnegie Institution of Washington by John Bolles. THE TEMPLE OF THE WALL PANELS, CHICHEN ITZA (1931) by Karl Ruppert describes the temple, the stairway of which appears in the foreground.

The sculptured motif is from the east doorway of the east wing.

CHICHEN ITZA
The Monjas

WHEN architecture of Mexican derivation was introduced at Chichen Itza, the earlier buildings still remained in use, and a number of closely knit groups are compounded of both styles. The Monjas, an important structure even in late times, is purely Maya in character. Its history goes back probably to the founding of the city, for in the days of the transition it was already ancient, having been altered and rebuilt several times. Within its massive substructure are at least two earlier platforms similar in design, each successive stage an enlargement of the original plan. The earlier temples, however, probably had only one story, for the latest additions seem designed expressly for the accommodation of the upper stairway. To the left of the Monjas is a small structure known as the Iglesia, also a Maya building. Its roof comb, decorated with masks, rises directly over the front wall, forming a sort of flying façade, a feature not unusual in the Puuc region, though more rare than the centrally placed type. In the foreground, the stairway leading to the Temple of the Wall Panels is sharply contrasting in style. The sloping base of the building wall, the serpent heads decorating the stairway, and the stone banner-holders are traits typically Mexican. Centered at some distance in front is a small square platform, almost exactly like the platforms near the Castillo, which Bishop Landa tells us were used for the performance of "plays and comedies to divert the people."

It is still uncertain when the radical changes reflected in the architecture of Chichen Itza took place. There is a date inscribed on one of the stone lintels of the Monjas, but it is recorded in the abbreviated fashion common in Yucatan, and authorities do not agree on its interpretation. According to the system of reading proposed by J. E. S. Thompson, now widely though not as yet universally accepted, this date falls in A.D. 880, and if this is correct, all dates associated with the Maya period at Chichen Itza fall within the twenty-year period between 866 and 886, in the era of the decline of the classic southern

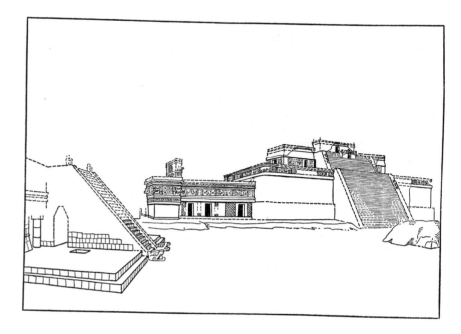

Maya culture. The only date which may pertain to the Mexican period is 998, more than a century later. It seems probable, therefore, that the change in Yucatan was a repercussion of the same extensive calamity that overtook the southern Maya cities. Here it did not result in such a decisive eclipse of civilization, but the weakening of the Maya tradition opened the way for a temporary rise of a hybrid culture, which was magnificent while it lasted, but which in turn was to be destroyed before it could push its frontiers far beyond the immediate environs of its capital.

23

CHICHEN ITZA, YUCATAN

The Red House

For THE Red House, see the cited publications of the Government of Mexico. THE CARACOL AT CHICHEN ITZA, YUCATAN, MEXICO (1935) by Karl Ruppert describes the structure in the background.

The serpent head is from the stairway leading to the Caracol.

CHICHEN ITZA
The Red House

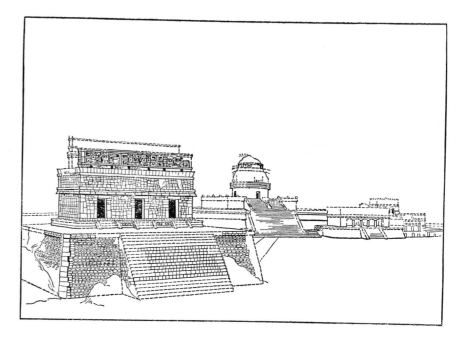

The RED HOUSE or Casa Colorada, sometimes called the Chichanchob, is not in fact red now, and it is questionable that its exterior was ever colored red, the name apparently being derived from traces of a red dado still visible on the interior. It is a Maya building, very much like the Monjas and the Iglesia. Its design is simple, almost severe, and ornament is concentrated on the flying façade and the taller roof comb behind it. A peculiar circumstance about this roof comb leaves its restoration open to doubt. At Chichen Itza, with the inception of the Mexican period, roof combs became obsolete, and sculptured elements—roof adornos—forming a parapet on the edge of the roof took their place. Several fragments of such adornos are scattered at the base of the Red House, and one, complete and unbroken, now lies partly buried in the debris of the comb on the roof itself. Unless for some unaccountable reason it had been deliberately carried and placed there when the roof comb was beginning to fall, it must have been somehow incorporated in the design, possibly in the course of repairs and alterations on the building during the period of Mexican influence. Excavation in the debris on the roof should determine whether there are other adornos, and whether they did form a feature of the design. In this restoration, a row of ornaments has been placed on top of the roof comb, but the solution seems stylistically improbable and has no precedent in Maya design. It is resorted to only because, however unsatisfactory, it seems to fit the observed facts better than any other.

The structure in the background is best known as the Caracol, a Spanish word for shell and, by extension, for a spiral stairway. Although the name probably derives from such a stairway mounting to a small upper chamber inside the building, it has sometimes been mistranslated as The House of the Snail. The building is also referred to as The Observatory in the belief that windows of the upper chamber were deliberately oriented to permit certain astronomical observations, but this is difficult to prove, now that most of the upper story has fallen. It has also been suggested that the Caracol may have served as a signal- or watchtower.

As questionable as the manner of its use are its stylistic affiliations. It has been assigned by some students to a postulated period of transition between purely Maya and Mexican forms. Others, however, stress its similarity to round structures at Mayapan, belonging to a much later period. There are two decipherable dates on sculptures at the Caracol, one in A.D. 886, the other in 968. They seem to favor the transitional hypothesis, but dates, of course, may not always have referred to the year in which they were inscribed, and the Maya so often re-used old sculpture in new constructions, that the evidence remains inconclusive. Only the discovery of stratigraphic relations between the Caracol and neighboring buildings, which may be made evident by the overlapping of floors in the plaza between them, could finally and decisively resolve the question.

24
CHICHEN ITZA, YUCATAN

Platforms on the North Terrace

SEE PREVIOUSLY cited monographs of the Ministry of Public Education of Mexico.

The jaguar holding a human heart is from the Platform of the Eagles.

CHICHEN ITZA
Platforms on the North Terrace

BISHOP LANDA mentions plays and comedies which the Maya performed for diversion, and describes two platforms near the Castillo which he says were theaters designed for such performances. These "theaters" are doubtless the so-called Temple of the Cones, which is not in fact a temple at all but a small square platform with four stairways, and a similar structure variously known as Mausoleum no. 1, the Tomb of the Chac Mool, and the Temple or Platform of the Eagles (Las Aguilas). The last name seems most apt, for its panels depict alternately eagles and jaguars, each holding what appears to be a human heart. Since eagles and jaguars were symbols of military orders in Yucatan, it seems not unlikely that the performances staged on these platforms were in some way connected with the ignoble art of waging war, which through Mexican influence was evidently gaining importance as a sphere of activity.

The platform to the right of the Eagles is called the Tzompantli, and suggests practices even more barbaric. Tzompantli is a Mexican word designating a wooden rack on which skulls of sacrificed prisoners were publicly displayed, and it was given to this platform because its lateral wings depict rows and tiers of human skulls impaled on stakes. Eagles are again portrayed on its eastern wing, together with many snakes and grim figures of emaciated warriors holding severed human heads. Skulls are not rare motifs in Maya art and human sacrifice was occasionally depicted, but they are usually executed with dignified restraint; there is nothing in earlier sculptures to compare with this rude and vigorous portrayal of a practice that reflects not the piety of sacrifice but the vengeful intent of mass execution of enemies and the preservation of their heads as trophies of war. It is entirely out of character with the serenity which characterizes the art of the great or "classic" period, and serves to demonstrate how the impact of two widely different cultures had changed the tenor of life in northern Yucatan, transforming its peaceful civilization into one militantly aggressive, and plunging the country into an era of strife and bloodshed.

25
CHICHEN ITZA, YUCATAN
The North Colonnade

A STUDY of this colonnade is included in THE TEMPLE OF THE WARRIORS AT CHICHEN ITZA, YUCATAN 1931) by Earl H. Morris, Jean Charlot, and Ann Axtell Morris.

The chac mool was excavated by Augustus Le Plongeon from the Platform of the Eagles.

CHICHEN ITZA
The North Colonnade

IN PUUC architecture, round columns, either monolithic or made up of several drums, had been used successfully to widen doorways which otherwise were restricted in size by their stone lintels, but the column was never regarded as an adequate support for the vault itself, and it never served to solve the problem of attaining larger room space within the building. It was the architects of the later period at Chichen Itza who first fully realized the advantages of the principle of concentrated support, and by its application created a new type of structure with room space no longer limited in width by a single span. By using the column as a structural support, they could span a room with several parallel vaults, permitting free circulation inside and providing ample lighting from the colonnaded façade. The use of the wooden lintel, with which they were already familiar, allowed a span large enough to make the construction spacious as well as practicable. Unfortunately this development came late in Maya history, and perhaps because of this, there never were worked out such standardized canons of form and proportion as characterized the orders of classical Old World architecture. The Maya used the simplest possible columns, one square in section, and the other round with a rectangular capital. They were built up of drums or blocks and, although the round drums were sometimes convex in section, there seem to have been no fixed rules of entasis or other refinements. When decoration was applied, it was simply carving on the surface of the column, or painting in horizontal zones. Such specialized forms as serpent columns and atlantean supports are features of a different category, used only in the doorways of particular types of buildings.

The colonnade was a radical innovation and we may judge from the Group of the Thousand Columns that it gained great popularity at Chichen Itza. The north building of this assemblage abuts on the terrace of the Temple of the Warriors, and consists of five parallel vaults supported on the interior by round columns and on the façade by square piers. Along the rear wall runs a bench, interrupted by a rectangular carved altar. Two of the columns of the rear row, slightly smaller in section than the others, rest on this altar. In front of it lies

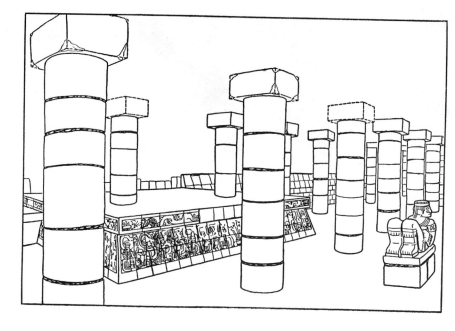

a chac mool. This is a type of statue not found in the southern Maya area, but common in many other regions from central Mexico to Costa Rica. It is a semirecumbent figure, lying in a preposterously uncomfortable position, with its head always sharply turned over one shoulder. It holds on its body a round disc or shallow basin, possibly a repository for offerings. The name Chac Mool, translated as Red Tiger, was first given by Augustus Le Plongeon to the statue he excavated from the fill of the Platform of the Eagles. To archaeologists, who unanimously reject Le Plongeon's fanciful reconstruction of the history of Chichen Itza, the name has ceased to have meaning, except as it now identifies a particular type of statue, the erratic distribution of which seems to point to the spread of a specific religious cult previously unknown among the Maya.

26

CHICHEN ITZA, YUCATAN

The Gallery of the Mercado

Karl Ruppert describes this building in detail in The Mercado, Chichen Itza, Yucatan (1943).

The motif is the central figure on the altar of the gallery.

CHICHEN ITZA
The Gallery of the Mercado

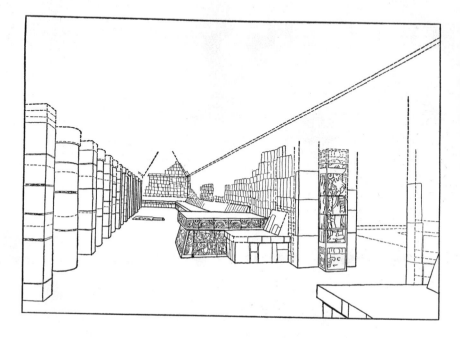

BERNAL DIAZ, who accompanied Cortez on his first entrance into Mexico City, was greatly impressed by its lively marketplace and described in detail the variety of goods bought and sold and the arrangement of the shops and other buildings on the plaza. The Group of the Thousand Columns at Chichen Itza vividly recalls this description, and was probably a similar center of trade for Yucatan. When some of the debris was cleared away, the floor of the court showed numerous traces of small constructions that may well have served as temporary booths for the selling of wares. It would seem, therefore, that the name "Mercado" (market) is more appropriate to the open court than to the building to which it is actually applied. This building, however, does face directly on the court, and may have been connected in function with the market. It has been suggested that it was something in the nature of a court-house, presided over by the judges who, according to many early accounts, were assigned to settle disputes arising from commercial transactions.

The building has a characteristic plan, which clearly defines a type so far identified only in buildings of the Mexican period of Chichen Itza. It consists of a long front gallery with a small court surrounded by a peristyle at the rear. The façade of the Mercado is a colonnade of alternating rectangular piers and round columns, so that the gallery is open to the court. These piers and columns were painted in bands of contrasting color, and probably the whole façade was treated in similar polychrome. The color scheme was apparently changed each time the building was repainted and it is now difficult to correlate all the scattered bits of color that remain. On the rear wall of the gallery, traces of design suggest that the motif was an undulating serpent, very similar to one depicted on a mural in the Temple of the Chac Mool, buried beneath the Temple of the Warriors. The panel above the altar or dais is, unfortunately, quite destroyed, but the dais itself is sculptured as well as painted, and still preserves much of its original color. This design shows a central figure sup-

ported in triumph by two recumbent or fallen men. On each side is a row of elaborately garbed prisoners tied together by a rope that binds their wrists, and near the head of each prisoner appears a symbol that doubtless explained his identity. The symbols do not resemble Maya hieroglyphs, and are more reminiscent of the place names recorded in the Mexican codices, though no parallels have been discovered for the individual characters. The whole suggests a symbolic portrayal of the subjugation of towns and chieftains, and the triumph of the cult of Kukulcan, represented by the writhing serpent.

27

CHICHEN ITZA, YUCATAN

The Patio of the Mercado

SEE KARL RUPPERT'S THE MERCADO, CHICHEN ITZA, YUCATAN (1943).

The feathered serpents are from the altar of the gallery.

CHICHEN ITZA
The Patio of the Mercado

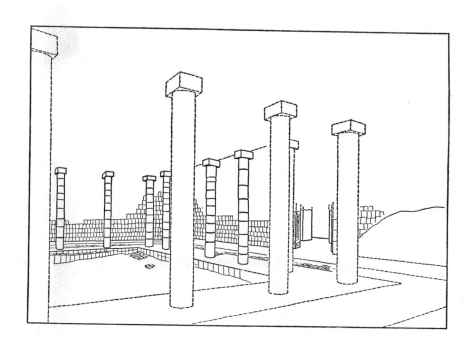

PASSING through the wide central doorway in the rear wall of the gallery, one enters a sort of ambulatory or patio built around a small interior court. This court is about a foot and a half below the level of the floor of the ambulatory and the step serves as a stylobate for tall slender columns arranged in the form of a peristyle. A flagged walk runs behind the colonnade, and high walls, with no openings save the doorway to the gallery, surround it on all sides. The roof probably was a thatch of palm leaves or grass laid over a framework of wooden poles, which in burning left the stones of the walls and the flagging discolored and cracked. We do not know just how the framework was constructed, but probably the ancient builders followed much the same principles in roofing their houses as the Maya do today. Ordinarily, the chief structural member is an A-shaped frame which rests on beams and supports the ridgepole and the main purlins. The common rafters are thin poles carrying horizontal rods which hold the thatch. No nails or pegs are used, and all members are securely lashed together with vines, maguey fibers, or strips of bark. The pitch of such a roof is usually steep to prevent the lifting of the thatch by the wind, and to allow a rapid runoff for the torrential rains. The Maya of today seldom confront problems as complex as those involved in the roofing of a large masonry structure such as the patio of the Mercado, but there is reason to think that the ancient builders, who had superior techniques of masonry construction, were equally skilled in the handling of wood, and were quite capable of solving such problems, for instance, as the adequate lining of roof gutters or the design of the juncture between the masonry roof of the gallery and the thatch of the patio. Flagstones set in the corners of the court reinforced the plaster floor just at the place where the runoff from the roof would be heaviest, and there is a general slope toward the two drains which lead through the stylobate and under the floor of the ambulatory to the outside.

What is most unusual in the design of the patio is its height and spaciousness. It is the only known example of Maya architecture which has columns approaching in proportion those of the classical orders. Their unusual slenderness, however, is not accompanied by any refinement of form. They are built, in fact, somewhat carelessly, of drums varying in diameter and evidently from some dismantled earlier building. The irregularity was afterward concealed with a thick coat of plaster. Even the arrangement of the columns is peculiar. The court is approximately square and the corner columns are slightly thicker than the others. Between them on the north, the west, and the south sides, there are five columns, but on the east side there are six. Perhaps excavation on that side would reveal some reason for this singular departure from symmetry.

UAXACTUN, GUATEMALA

Structure A-V

A DETAILED STUDY of this structure, including a report on its excavation, is being prepared by A. Ledyard Smith and Robert E. Smith for the Carnegie Institution of Washington. The following plates were originally designed for this study and are reproduced here by courtesy of its authors.

The monument is Stela 26.

UAXACTUN
Structure A-V

THE EXCAVATION of a building follows its history in reverse. An archaeologist first sees the abandoned ruin, half-buried in its own debris and overgrown with vegetation. As the debris, which serves to protect what it covers, is cleared away, better-preserved portions of the structure are revealed and he can then more clearly visualize it as it appeared before its abandonment. After he has made a thorough study of the details of its construction, he usually discovers that some parts are earlier than others, and, trenching through the walls of the substructures or foundations, he may discover still older constructions entirely overlaid by masonry, and under these, even more ancient walls. Thus, through successive strata, he follows back the sequence of events into a distant past. However, we find it easier to follow time in a forward direction. Structure A-V is here presented in the order of its growth, to show how it changed gradually, in style, manner of construction, orientation, and even in its essential function, from its modest beginning as a compact group of small temples to its imposing aspect as the most important palace group at Uaxactun.

The accompanying sketch is schematic and shows the standing portions of the ruin cut by a central trench. The cross sections are indicated in solid black, and successive stages are set back to the right to make clear their relation to underlying phases. The drawing has been simplified by the omission of all but the most important modifications of the cross section. Other parts of the building are shown in their latest phase, and ruined portions are indicated by light stippling.

The stages as they are depicted are numbered consecutively, but as they do not take account of all the minor sequences of building activity, several consecutive alterations are in some cases grouped in a single drawing. Mr. A. Ledyard Smith, who was in charge of excavations and who has made a thorough study of this structure, has worked out, for the detailed final report, a more comprehensive scheme of building sequences, which includes early phases not covered in this study, and relates each phase to the larger periods of Maya history, as they are reflected in differences of ceramic wares and in fundamental improvements of building technique. Until the final publication of his study, designations must be regarded as tentative, but the following correlation of the principal periods is included with Mr. Smith's kind permission:

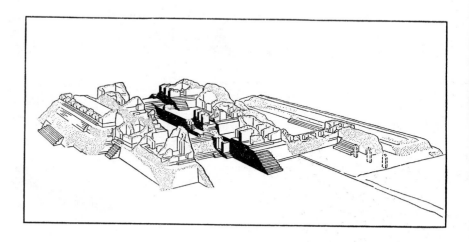

CULTURAL PERIOD	ARCHITECTURAL PHASE		STAGE DEPICTED
Early Developmental	Pre-masonry (not represented in Structure A-V		
Late Developmental	Pre-vault (Subphases a to f)		
Early Classic	Phase I of the vault:	Ia	
		Ib	
		Ic	Stage 1
		Id	
		Ie	
		If	Stage 2
		Ig	Stage 3
		Ih	Stage 4
Late Classic	Phase II of the vault:	IIa	Stage 5
		IIb	
		IIc	Stage 6
		IId	Stage 7
		IIe	
		IIf	
		IIg	
		IIh	Stage 8

28
Structure A-V, Stage 1

Originally, perhaps when the city of Uaxactun was as yet only a village, the site of Structure A-V was occupied by a number of small house-platforms. One such platform, discovered beneath the substructure at the level of the plaza floor, was almost perfectly preserved. It had rounded ends, and post holes in the floor showed that it once had supported a three-room house, also with rounded ends and with a small rectangular porch. Although it was prominently located and must have been quite important in the community, it seems to have no specific relation to the first formally arranged masonry structure later erected on the same spot. This is a larger, rectangular platform, ascended from the south by a very broad stairway with a small room on each side. On this platform, facing the center, stand three vaulted temples almost exactly alike. Each con-tains two small rooms with absurdly high and narrow vaults made of crudely shaped stones laid in thick joints of mortar. The masonry is so rough that inches of plaster applied to its surface fail to hide its irregularity. Walls are un-decorated, and the stucco ornament and the tall roof combs are reconstructions suggested by other known buildings of the same type. These early temples are not raised on high, pyramidal substructures, but in every other respect they re-semble the more spectacular "pyramid-temples" of later periods, even to the characteristic platforms, closely following the outline of the building plan. There is no doubt that they were built for the worship of gods—of some tribal trinity whose names and attributes we shall probably never know, but whose power to inspire men to effort is attested by later events.

29
Structure A-V, Stage 2

While the three temples were still in use, a great priest or chieftain died in the city, and elaborate preparations were made for his funeral. Builders erected small masonry structures in front of the temple steps, roofed, or draped with awnings supported on posts, the whole court, and constructed in the center a crypt for the interment of the body. The ceremonies were impressive and lasted for many days. Afterwards, the temporary structures were not razed to the ground but carelessly torn down, and the remains were covered with masonry, raising the level of the court floor to the doorsills of the temples. A small open platform in the middle of the court probably served for periodic rites in memory of the deceased. The south stairway, too, was elaborated, and above it was placed a carved monument, Stela 26, bearing the Maya date 9.0.10.0.0, A.D. 445. This is the first sound evidence of the age of these constructions, giving us a chance to estimate with some accuracy how long a period of time is represented in the history of their development.

30
Structure A-V, Stage 3

A bit of historical drama is suggested by the events that followed the erection of Stela 26. Most fortunately, the date on the back was not touched, but all the carving on the face was carefully chipped or ground off, and only the deepest lines were left, sketching the rough contours of a human figure that originally stood out in fairly high relief. It is interesting to speculate on the motives that prompted such deliberate mutilation of the sculpture. Did some enemy or rival of the personage commemorated by the stela jealously replace the portrait by another, painted on plaster, or was the statue imbued with dangerous powers to bring vengeance on the apostates who dared to bury it intact? We know that it did not stand exposed for many years. Immediately, or very soon afterward, a platform was built around it, covering it and extending the level of the main court to accommodate a small shrine. Access to the court is now through this shrine, which has doorways facing both the court and the stairway. One can imagine that before the three main temples may be approached, some ceremony of purification, some obeisance or offering is demanded, possibly as a penance for the act of vandalism perpetrated on a sacred image.

31
Structure A-V, Stage 4

About sixty years have passed since the erection of the now buried stela, and another important funeral has taken place. One of the small rooms at the side of the main stairway has been utilized as a burial chamber, and its doorway is sealed with masonry. Two more shrines have been built, and standing in the rear room of the shrine on the left is a stela inscribed with the date 9.3.10.0.0 (A.D. 504). In effect the new shrines now screen from view the court of the three original temples. No longer can the casual passerby on the plaza observe freely the ceremonies being performed before the temple steps. Apparently, the ritual has become not only more elaborate but more esoteric as well. Probably already, in other parts of the city, larger and more imposing temples are being built to supersede this humble group, for there is to be no further elaboration of its religious function. Later changes take an entirely new direction.

32
Structure A-V, Stage 5

Radical changes in building plan and masonry technique inaugurate a new era of culture, an era of prosperity that flowers in intense building activity everywhere, in finer sculpture, and in further advances in astronomical knowledge. There is a closer affinity now between all Maya cities, and one can also sense a closer integration of the secular and the religious aspects of society, as if the growing power of the astronomer-priests is encroaching upon the functions of civil government, or, on the other hand, as if the ruling families begin to assume the prerogatives of priestly office. Something of the sort is vaguely reflected in the form of the new structure that now completely covers the original

south stairway of the group. It is a type of building we usually associate with civic or residential functions. There are three rooms opening on the plaza, and two smaller rooms with interior doorways. The roof of the building forms a broad terrace in front of the three shrines. It probably had a low parapet, which has been reconstructed on the basis of carved elements found re-used in a later stairway but obviously designed originally to stand vertically as roof ornaments. A small, one-room building against the west shrine is the first unit built on the western façade, which continues to grow in importance, as more stelae are erected on the main plaza which it faces.

33
Structure A-V, Stage 6

The trend which began in the previous stage continues to gather momentum. New additions are ever more ambitious and more secular in character. The large palace that now replaces the rear temple is the most imposing structure yet attempted, and looks more like a residence of some very important personage than like a purely formal building. Several such buildings in the group contain traces of fires and bits of household pottery wares, and burials associated with them include remains of women and children, in contrast to the earlier temple burials which are invariably of adult men. In one of the rooms is a drawing of a building with a parapet of T-shaped elements, which is very helpful as a model for the restoration of the roof. The new palace is approached not only from the court, but also by a broad stairway on the north. In this stage it is difficult to tell which is the principal façade of the group as a whole. Later, however, the north stairway is first narrowed and finally entirely covered by terraces, and its temporary importance in the composition is not maintained.

34
Structure A-V, Stage 7

For a long time the group has been expanding. The most striking change is the complete rebuilding of the south façade and the formation of a second court in front of the three shrines by a large U-shaped palace that faces on the plaza. Important changes, too, appear in construction and design. Cut masonry is now a shallow veneer on the surface of the walls, and solid parapets replace the daintier carved elements of earlier periods. It may be worth while to note that the group now has approaches on all sides and that the west façade has been elaborated by the addition of several rooms and two new stairways. Narrow steps lead to the roof of one of the west buildings, so that it can serve as an open terrace. We can safely assume that the intensity of the tropical sun over Uaxactun rules out the possibility of anything like our cult of sun-bathers, but we might venture to guess that since new architectural additions have restricted the view of the sky within the narrow courts, the astronomer-priest may come here after nightfall to study the heavenly bodies.

35
Structure A-V, Stage 8

In its final stage Structure A-V is a complicated arrangement of courts surrounded by palaces built on different levels. Only one of the ancient temples still survives, almost hidden and completely hemmed in by newer structures. Most of the buildings are severely rectangular in plan, and even the three shrines have been incorporated in a single structure that separates the two upper courts. The latest developments are centered on the east court, formed by a long mound that is bare of any superstructure. It looks unfinished, as if the work that had been carried on here for many centuries was suddenly interrupted in the midst of sanguine plans for expansion. We are facing again the enigma of the mysterious events that are soon to sweep into oblivion all the great cities of the Maya Old Empire, for the crucial years of decline have left no monuments to reveal the nature of their agonies.

36

UAXACTUN, GUATEMALA
Groups A and B

THE CARNEGIE INSTITUTION OF WASH-INGTON carried on excavations at Uaxactun from 1926 to 1940, and reports on individual structures appear in its various publications. Intensive architectural studies in Groups A and B have been made under the direction of A. Ledyard Smith, and this reconstruction is based largely on as yet unpublished data made available by him for this study. A good general description of the site of Uaxactun is given in THE INSCRIPTIONS OF PETEN (1937-1938) by Sylvanus G. Morley.

The jade figurine is from Structure A-18 at Uaxactun.

UAXACTUN
Groups A and B

LOOKING toward Structure A-V from a more remote point of view, we can see its central position in a larger setting, among the palaces and temples of Groups A and B, which comprise what is sometimes called the Acropolis of Uaxactun. The city is built on a terrain of low hills separated by more or less level areas. There are eight principal monumental groups erected on the summits of the hills, which had been in part cut down and in part built up to form broad level plazas. The intervening ground, where it is not too steeply sloping or too low to avoid inundation during the rainy seasons, was occupied by residential buildings and minor plazas and courts, but no attempt has been made to restore these little-known sections of the city, for the amount of excavation undertaken in the house-mound areas so far has been insufficient to determine precisely their extent and arrangement. The apparent isolation of the monumental groups in the surrounding forest is therefore somewhat misleading, though it must be remembered that so far as we know the Maya never disposed their habitations formally in streets or crowded them unduly in congested areas. Even within the confines of a city, each household was probably set apart at some distance from its neighbors, and it is a common trait of the Maya cities of the Old Empire that they have no well-defined limits, but tend to cover a large area of gradually thinning occupation, sometimes on the outskirts merging with neighboring communities which may have been independent towns or merely suburban centers.

The eight groups of Uaxactun lie close together and are connected with each other by paved roads, artificially raised as they pass over low areas. The road between Groups A and B follows a natural ridge between the two hills. An opening in its low parapet on the left side gives access to a rectangular reservoir, which was probably very necessary during the dry season to preserve a supply of water. In the foreground at the left is a depression which probably was another reservoir. Immediately behind it, a deep dump of potsherds and other debris suggests that the builders of Uaxactun intended eventually to extend the terraces in this direction. Now it provides a rich source of material

for the ceramicist, whose study of the imperishable remains of the almost universal craft of pottery making is an invaluable aid to the archaeologist in his reconstruction of ancient history.

The buildings of Uaxactun are, unfortunately, in a deplorable state of decay. Many which have not been excavated appear on the surface to be nothing but formless mounds of debris. But the greater their ruin, the greater an incentive it is to the archaeologist to wrest from them the secrets they still hold. In his efforts to reconstruct the social background of the Maya, he is pitting his clumsy and laborious methods, which often seem discouragingly unrewarding against the slow but efficient and inexorable processes of nature. In this unequal contest he can hope only for minor victories, but victories nevertheless valuable and permanent, for no new discovery, however trifling, about his past can be subtracted from man's almost imperceptibly growing awareness of himself and of the universe about him.